...uide

Adobe®
Photoshop®
Elements 4.0

MACINTOSH

Adobe

Contents

Chapter 1: Getting Started

Installation and registration. 1

Adobe Help Center 1

Using Help 3

Tips and training 6

New features 7

Chapter 2: Tutorials

Tutorial 1: Learn the workflow. 9

Tutorial 2: Edit your photos 10

Chapter 3: Photoshop Elements workspace

About workspaces. 15

How Tos, context menus, and shortcuts 18

Tools. 20

Palettes and bins 22

Viewing images in the Editor. 25

Rulers and the grid (Editor only). . . . . ❓

Undo, redo, and cancel 29

Presets and libraries (Editor only). 31

Scratch disks and plug-ins . . . . ❓

Chapter 4: Using Adobe Bridge

The basics of Bridge 33

Files and folders in Bridge. 35

Managing Bridge . . . . ❓

Chapter 5: Opening and saving files

Acquiring image files 41

Opening files. 41

Working with metadata. . . . . ❓

❓ Indicates a topic that appears only in Help

Saving and exporting images 43
Processing camera raw image files 45

Chapter 6: Using Layers
Creating layers 47
Editing layers. 50
Copying and arranging layers . . . . ❓
Opacity and blending modes . . . . ❓
Adjustment and fill layers. . . . . ❓
Layer groups . . . . ❓

Chapter 7: Selecting parts of an image
Making selections 53
Modifying selections 62
Smoothing selection edges with anti-aliasing and feathering . . . . ❓
Moving and copying selections 64
Saving selections. . . . . ❓

Chapter 8: Correcting and understanding color
Color correction basics 67
Adjusting shadows and light. 72
Correcting color casts 74
Adjusting color saturation and hue. 75
Setting press target values. . . . . ❓
Understanding color . . . . ❓
Using image modes and color tables. . . . . ❓
Setting up color management . . . . ❓

Chapter 9: Cropping and resizing photos
Cropping. 77
Image size and resolution. 81

Chapter 10: Retouching and transforming
Retouching 87
Transforming. 90

❓ Indicates a topic that appears only in Help

Chapter 11: Using filters, effects, and styles

Filters, effects, and layer styles 93

Layer styles and effects . . . . ❓

Filters . . . . ❓

Adjustment filters . . . . ❓

Artistic filters . . . . ❓

Blur filters . . . . ❓

Brush Stroke filters . . . . ❓

Distort filters . . . . ❓

Noise filters . . . . ❓

Pixelate filters . . . . ❓

Render filters . . . . ❓

Sharpen filters . . . . ❓

Sketch filters . . . . ❓

Stylize filters . . . . ❓

Texture filters . . . . ❓

Video filters . . . . ❓

Other filters . . . . ❓

Chapter 12: Painting

Painting overview 97

Choosing colors . . . . ❓

Painting tools . . . . ❓

Setting up brushes . . . . ❓

Fills and strokes . . . . ❓

Patterns . . . . ❓

Gradients . . . . ❓

Chapter 13: Adding text and shapes

Adding and editing text 99

Asian type . . . . ❓

Creating shapes 99

Editing shapes . . . . ❓

Optimizing for the web and e-mail

Optimizing images . . . . ❓

Using transparency and mattes . . . . ❓

Dithering in web images. . . . . ❓

Previewing web images . . . . ❓

Chapter 14: Printing and sharing photos

Printing photos. 101

Print options . . . . ❓

Sharing your photos. . . . . ❓

Keyboard shortcuts

Editor workspace keyboard shortcuts . . . . ❓

Adobe Bridge keyboard shortcuts. . . . . ❓

Glossary

Photoshop Elements Glossary . . . . ❓

Glossary. . . . . ❓

Index 113

❓ Indicates a topic that appears only in Help

Chapter 1: Getting Started

Installation and registration

To install

1 Close any applications that are open.

2 Insert the product CD or DVD into your computer's disc drive.

3 After the Autoplay screen appears, follow the on-screen instructions. (If the Autoplay screen doesn't appear, double-click the CD or DVD icon on your desktop.)

For more detailed instructions about installing the software and installing an upgrade, see the How To Install file on the product CD or DVD. For a list of system requirements, see the product page on the Adobe website. For details about the permitted number of computers on which you can install the software, see the license agreement included with the software.

Note: To uninstall the product, use the Add Or Remove Programs utility in Windows®.

To register

Register your Adobe product to receive complimentary support on installation and product defects and notifications about product updates.

❖ Do one of the following:

• Install the software to access the Registration dialog box, and then follow the on-screen instructions. An active Internet connection is required.

• Complete the PDF registration card on the product CD or DVD and return it to the address indicated.

Adobe Help Center

About Adobe Help Center

Adobe® Help Center is a free, downloadable application that includes three primary features.

Product Help Provides Help for Adobe desktop products installed on your system. (If no Adobe desktop products are installed, topics for them aren't available.) Help topics are updated periodically and can be downloaded through Adobe Help Center preferences. For the products you've installed, Product Help also provides dynamic listings of the top support issues and the most recent support documents published on Adobe.com.

Expert Support Provides information about Adobe Expert Support plans and lets you store details about plans you've purchased. If you have an active support plan, you can also use the Expert Support section to submit web cases—questions sent to Adobe support professionals over the web. To access links in the Expert Support section, you must have an active Internet connection.

More Resources Provides easy access to the extensive resources on Adobe.com, including support pages, user forums, tips and tutorials, and training. You can also use this area to store contact information for friends, colleagues, or support professionals, or even websites you turn to for inspiration or troubleshooting information.

To check for updates

Adobe periodically provides updates to software and to topics in Adobe Help Center. You can easily obtain these updates through Adobe Help Center. An active Internet connection is required.

1 Click the Preferences button in the top-right corner.

2 In the Preferences dialog box, click Check For Updates. If updates are available, follow the on-screen directions to download and save them.

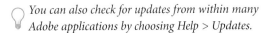 *You can also check for updates from within many Adobe applications by choosing Help > Updates.*

To set Adobe Help Center preferences

1 Click the Preferences button in the top-right corner.

2 Set any of the following options, and click OK.

Region Specifies your geographical location. Changing this option may affect which services are available to you.

Language Specifies the language in which Expert Support content is displayed.

Display Renewal Reminders For Expert Support Contracts Displays reminder screens when your Expert Support plan has almost expired. Deselect this option if you'd like to turn off these reminders.

Enable Auto Login For Web Case Submission Allows you to submit support questions over the web. This option is available only if you have an active Expert Support plan.

User Interface Language Specifies the language in which Adobe Help Center interface text is displayed.

Check For Updates Searches for new updates to software and Help topics as they become available from Adobe. This option also lets you specify notification options and choose which applications to update.

Network Administrators Displays options for network administration.

To view support documents

From within Adobe Help Center, you can get up-to-the-minute listings of the top support issues and the most recent documents added to the support knowledgebase. Each time you start Adobe Help Center, it uses RSS (Really Simple Syndication) technology to gather this information from the Adobe website and update the listings dynamically.

1 In Adobe Help Center, click Product Help and select a product from the For menu.

2 Click the Contents tab in the navigation pane, and do either of the following:

- Click Recent Documents to display a summary of the most recent documents for the selected product.

- Click Top Issues to display a summary of the top issues documents for the selected product.

3 To view a document in full on the Adobe website, click its link. (An active Internet connection is required.)

To display More Resources

The More Resources section in Adobe Help Center provides easy access to some of the content and services available from the Adobe website, including support, training, tutorials, and forums.

❖ To display this section, click More Resources.

To add contact information in More Resources

1 Click More Resources, and then click Personal Contacts.

2 Do any of the following:

- To add a contact, click New, type the contact information you want to save, and click OK.

- To edit a contact, click a contact in the list, click Edit, make changes to the information, and click OK.

- To delete a contact, click a contact in the list, and then click Delete. To confirm the deletion, click Yes.

Using Help

Using Help

The complete documentation for using your Adobe product is available in Help, a browser-based system you can access through Adobe Help Center. Help topics are updated periodically, so you can always be sure to have the most recent information available. For details, search for "check for updates" in Help.

Important: Adobe Help systems include all of the information in the printed user guides, plus additional information not included in print. A PDF version of the complete Help content, optimized for printing, is also provided on the CD or DVD in the product box.

To navigate Help

❖ Do any of the following:

- To view Help for a product, choose the product name from the For menu.

- To expand or collapse a section, click the blue triangle to the left of the section name.

- To display a topic, click its title.

To search Help topics

Search using words or phrases to quickly find topics. You can search Help for one product or for all Adobe products you've installed. If you find a topic that you may want to view again, bookmark it for quick retrieval.

1 In Adobe Help Center, click Product Help, and choose a product from the For menu.

2 Type one or more words in the Search For box, and choose an option from the In menu:

This Product Searches Help for the selected product.

All Products Searches Help for all Adobe products you have installed.

Search Help for one product or for all products you've installed

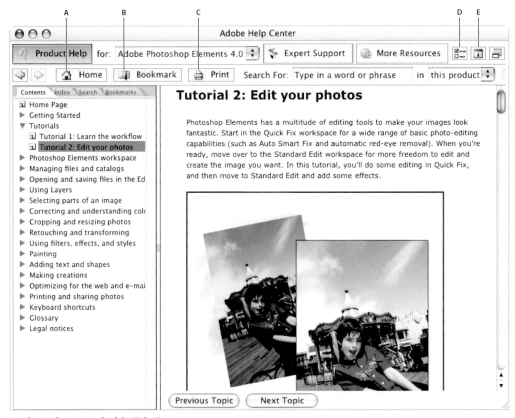

Product Help section of Adobe Help Center
*A. Returns you to Help home page **B.** Adds bookmark for current topic **C.** Prints contents of right pane **D.** Opens Preferences dialog box **E.** Opens About Adobe Help Center window*

3 Click Search. Topics matching the search words appear in the navigation pane, grouped by product and listed in order of relevance.

4 To view a topic, click its title.

5 To return to the navigation pane, do one of the following:

• Click the Home button.

• Click the Back button.

• Click Next Topic or Previous Topic.

Search tips

The search feature in Adobe Help Center works by searching the entire Help text for topics that contain any of the words typed in the Search For box. These tips can help you improve your search results in Help:

• If you search using a phrase, such as "shape tool," put quotation marks around the phrase. The search returns only those topics containing all words in the phrase.

• Make sure that the search terms are spelled correctly.

• If a search term doesn't yield results, try using a synonym, such as "web" instead of "Internet."

To print a topic from Help

1 Select the topic you want to print, and click the Print button.

2 Choose the printer you'd like to use, and then click Print.

To change the view

By default, Adobe Help Center opens in Full view. Full view gives you access to the Product Help, Expert Support, and More Resources sections. Switch to Compact view when you want to see only the selected Help topic and you want to keep the Help window on top of your product workspace.

❖ Click the view icon 🗗 to switch between Full and Compact views.

To use bookmarks

You can bookmark especially helpful topics for easy access, just as you bookmark pages in a web browser, and reread them at another time.

• To view bookmarks, click the Bookmarks tab in the navigation pane.

• To create a bookmark, select the topic you want to mark, and click the Bookmark button 📖. When the New Bookmark dialog box appears, type a new name in the text box if desired, and then click OK.

• To delete a bookmark, select it in the Bookmarks pane, and click the Delete button. Click Yes to confirm the deletion.

• To rename a bookmark, select it in the Bookmarks pane, and then click the Rename Bookmark button 📝. In the dialog box, type a new name for the bookmark and then click OK.

• To move a bookmark, select it in the Bookmarks pane, and then click the Move Up button 🔼 or the Move Down button 🔽.

Tips and training

Learning resources

Adobe provides a wide range of resources to help you learn and use Adobe products.

- Tutorials: Short step-by-step lessons that guide you through workflows to produce end results and help you learn the software.

- How Tos: A collection of quick procedures to help you complete common tasks.

- Support: Complimentary and paid technical support options from Adobe.

- Other resources: Training, books, user forums, product certification, and more.

- Extras: Downloadable content and software.

Tutorials

The Help system includes several step-by-step tutorials on key features and concepts. These tutorials are also available in the complete, printable, PDF version of Help, included on the product CD or DVD.

To use these tutorials with the product, select the tutorial you want from the Contents pane in Adobe Help Center, and click the View icon to switch to Compact view. Compact view keeps the Help window on top of the application windows, regardless of what window or application is selected. Drag an edge or a corner of the Help window to resize it.

The Adobe website provides additional tutorials that take you beyond the basics, showing you special techniques and ways to produce professional results. You can access these tutorials from the product page on Adobe.com.

How Tos

How Tos are short sets of instructions that help you quickly complete common tasks. Some How Tos also contain links to related topics in Help.

To access How Tos, choose Window > How To, and then select a task set from the pop-up menu.

Other resources

Additional sources of information and help are available for Adobe products.

- Visit the Training area of the Adobe website for access to Adobe Press books; online, video, and instructor-led training resources; Adobe software certification programs; and more.

- Visit the Adobe user forums, where users share tips, ask questions, and find out how others are getting the most out of their software. User forums are available in English, French, German, and Japanese on the main Support page of your local Adobe website.

- Visit the Support area of the Adobe website for additional information about free and paid technical support options. Top issues are listed by product on the Adobe U.S. and Adobe Japan websites.

- Click More Resources in Adobe Help Center to access many of the resources on the Adobe website and to create a custom list of user groups, websites, and contacts you frequently turn to for information.

Extras

The Downloads area of the Adobe website includes free updates, tryouts, and other useful software. In addition, the Plug-ins section of the Adobe Store provides access to thousands of plug-ins from third-party developers, helping you automate tasks, customize workflows, create specialized professional effects, and more.

New features

What's new

Quick Fix Use the newly enhanced automatic correction options for the most common photo flaws. (See "To correct color in Quick Fix" on page 67.)

Magic Selection Brush tool Easily and accurately select portions of your photos using this new tool in either Standard Edit and Quick Fix. Simply scribble or place dots on the object you want to select—no need to precisely outline the object—and Adobe Photoshop Elements selects the object for you. You can add to or subtract from the selection by using additional tools in the options bar. (See "To use the Magic Selection Brush tool" on page 58.)

Magic Extractor Easily select an object in a photo and extract it from its background. Just scribble or place dots on the object you want to extract; then scribble or place dots on the background, and Photoshop Elements separates the object from its background. This tool is perfect for creating composites or

scrapbook images. (See "To use the Magic Extractor" on page 60.)

Skin tone adjustment Click an area of skin and watch the tonal balance of all colors in the photo improve. If you want, you can also manually adjust the color by using color sliders. (See "To adjust the color of skin tone" on page 76.)

Red eye removal Easily remove red eye in either Standard Edit or Quick Fix. (See "To remove red eye" on page 87.)

Defringe Automatically remove the colored specs or halo around the edges of a selection. (See "To defringe a selection" on page 63.)

Straighten tool Straighten and crop crooked photos by drawing a horizontal or vertical line in the image. Photoshop Elements aligns the photo to that line. (See "To straighten an image" on page 80.)

WYSIWYG font menu What you see is what you get—see what each font looks like from within the font menu. (See "To choose a font family and style" in Help.)

What's changed

Crop tool Freely change image size boundaries while cropping an image. (See "To crop an image" on page 77.)

Paragraph text Create paragraph text by dragging a border with the Text tool. The text you enter inside the border wraps to remain inside the boundaries. (See "To add text" in Help.)

Easier color management Easily get the color you expect when printing. New options and improved embedded profile support streamline color management. (See "About color management" in Help.)

Advanced camera raw Fine tune exposure and lighting by working with the raw data from your digital camera, and easily export photos to the universal DNG format. (See "About camera raw image files" on page 45.)

Artifact reduction Quickly remove noise caused by shooting in low light or with ISO camera settings by using the new Remove JPEG Artifacts option in the Noise filter. (See "Reduce Noise" in Help.)

Chapter 2: Tutorials

Tutorial 1: Learn the workflow

Adobe® Photoshop® Elements provides a complete workflow solution for working with digital photos, by integrating a wide range of digital editing, sharing, and searching capabilities.

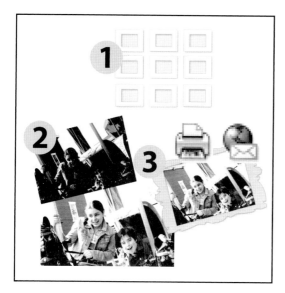

1. Import and organize your photos with Adobe Bridge.

Adobe Bridge is the perfect partner to Photoshop Elements. You can view, manage, and organize your photos all in one place. In Bridge, files display as thumbnails, making it easy for you to navigate to image files already on your computer.

If you have new photos on your digital camera, you can use Bridge to import them. Start Bridge, and then connect your camera to your computer. Click the Folders tab and browse to your camera (if it appears as a drive or a volume on your desktop). Make sure that the folder you want to add the photos to is open. Select the images on the camera, then drag them to the folder where you want to store them. That's how easy it is to get photos from your digital camera with Bridge.

2. Edit and enhance your photos.

From bad lighting to red eyes, Photoshop Elements can fix it. You edit your photos in one of the two Editor workspaces: Quick Fix or Standard Edit.

Use Quick Fix for simple fixes, such as removing red-eye, reducing shadows, or adjusting color. For more control and more options, use Standard Edit. The Standard Edit workspace has many of the same tools and features the professionals use, such as Levels, which lets you easily improve the lighting in a photo. Photoshop Elements editing tools give you full artistic license—you can use them to remove someone from a picture, create a composite of several pictures, or add wild effects.

3. Print and share your photos.

Choose File > Print to bring up the Print dialog box, where you can view a preview of a photo. Then click Print to enjoy your finished image.

If you enjoy sending photos to friends and family electronically, you can choose to have a photo automatically attached to an e-mail message. Click the

Attach to E-mail button in the shortcuts bar. Photoshop Elements helps you convert the photo to the JPEG format (typically the easiest file format for sharing), and then attaches the photo.

If you use a web-based e-mail system, Photoshop Elements may not be able to attach a photo. In this case, simply start your e-mail service, and then manually attach the photo.

Tutorial 2: Edit your photos

Photoshop Elements has a multitude of editing tools to make your images look fantastic. Start in the Quick Fix workspace for a wide range of basic photo-editing capabilities (such as Auto Smart Fix and automatic red-eye removal). When you're ready, move over to the Standard Edit workspace for more freedom to edit and create the image you want. In this tutorial, you'll do some editing in Quick Fix, and then move to Standard Edit and add some effects.

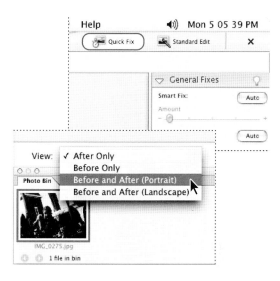

1. Open your photo in Quick Fix.

In Quick Fix, choose File > Open.

Choose Before And After from the View menu located at the lower left corner of the image area. This view sets up the Quick Fix workspace so that you can see both the original and the edited versions.

2. Adjust the lighting.

This photo is a little too dark and could use some lighting adjustments to bring out the details. To quickly and easily adjust the lighting, click the Auto button next to Smart Fix in the General Fixes palette. Photoshop Elements automatically adjusts the lighting. Drag the Amount slider to increase or decrease the amount of lighting adjustment applied. When you're satisfied, click the Commit button ✔ at the top of the General Fixes palette. Experiment with the other lighting and color settings as desired.

If you don't like the way a correction looks, choose Edit > Undo *[last edit]*. You can undo several steps, so don't hold back!

To see a color version of this image, see Figure 2-1 in the color section.

3. Open your photo in Standard Edit.

With the image still in the Quick Fix, click the Standard Edit button in the upper right corner of the window. The image opens in the Standard Edit window, which hosts a variety of editing tools, as well as a Layers palette for compositing other images and text onto your photo.

4. Adjust the color.

To bring out the natural skin tones in the people in the photo and enhance the colors for the entire photo, choose Enhance > Adjust Color > Adjust Color For Skin Tone. Click the boy's face (or a face in your own photo) using the eyedropper tool. Try clicking the girl's face to see the different results based on the original skin tone of each. To make further adjustments, drag the Skin sliders to increase or decrease the amount of tan or blush colors, or drag the Temperature slider to make the colors warmer (more red tones) or cooler (more blue tones). If your colors get too far from natural, click Reset to start over.

To see a color version of this image, see Figure 2-2 in the color section.

5. Remove flaws.

The Healing Brush tool and the Spot Healing Brush tool help you easily rid your photos of unflattering flaws such as blemishes, dark circles, and other distractions.

Use the Healing Brush tool for fixing large areas, such as a person's entire cheek. For example, to remove the red from ruddy cheeks, hold down the Option key and click in the non-red area of the person's face to sample color from that area. Then drag the Healing Brush over the red cheeks to paint the sampled color onto the red cheeks.

Use the Spot Healing Brush for small repairs, such as blemishes or small spots. You don't have to sample colors when using this tool—because it fixes a small area, it samples the colors around the tool pointer. For example, in the photo of the kids on the carousel, use this tool to remove the big white dot on the boy's red shirt. First zoom into the area by clicking the dot with Zoom In tool . Then select the Spot Healing brush in the toolbox and select 5 px from the Size menu in the options bar. Click the white button and—presto!—it's gone.

6. Add artistic effects.

Using the Zoom Out tool 🔍, set your image back to a normal viewing size. Now you'll add some artistic flair by applying filters.

In the Styles And Effects palette, choose Filters from the first menu and choose All from the second menu (these are the defaults, so they should already be selected). Scroll through the list of filters, and double-click Film Grain to open the options dialog box for that filter. Experiment with the options by setting Grain Size lower and higher. Once you've opened an options dialog box for one filter, you can choose other filters from within that dialog box and view their results. To apply the filter, click OK. Experiment with some different filters until you're satisfied with the result.

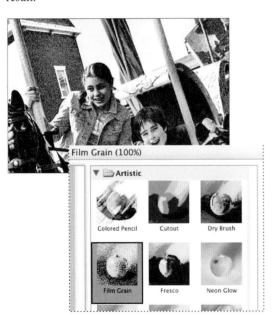

To see a color version of this image, see Figure 2-3 in the color section.

7. Add text and save your file.

Select the Type tool T in the toolbox, click anywhere in the photo, and type **San Francisco**. Drag to select all the text, and then, in the options bar, specify a font, style, size, and color. Next, to position the text on your photo, select the Move tool ➤⊕ in the toolbox and drag the text to center it in the top third of the photo. Notice that the text is on its own layer in the Layers palette so you can edit it independently from your background.

Choose File > Save. Name the file **Opening** and choose Photoshop (PSD) as the format. (The PSD format keeps the layers separate for future editing, rather than merging them as other formats do.) Choose File > Close.

To see a color version of this image, see Figure 2-4 in the color section.

Chapter 3: Photoshop Elements workspace

About workspaces

About the Welcome Screen

When you first start Photoshop Elements, the Welcome Screen opens by default. The Welcome Screen is a convenient starting point, or hub, for major tasks in Photoshop Elements.

Position the mouse pointer over an icon at the top of the window to see a description of the tasks that you can perform in each workspace. Click an icon to open the workspace for that task.

You can close or reopen the Welcome Screen at any time by choosing Window > Welcome. You do not need to return to the Welcome Screen to open other workspaces—you can open different workspaces from within any other workspace.

The Welcome Screen
A. Click a button to enter a specific workspace **B.** *List of recently opened images. Click a file name to open a photo.* **C.** *Deselect the Show at Startup option if you don't want the Welcome Screen to display when you launch Photoshop Elements.*

About Standard Edit

The Standard Edit workspace , also called the Editor, has tools to correct color problems, create special effects, and enhance photos.

If you've worked with images before, you'll find that the Standard Edit workspace provides a flexible and powerful image-correction environment. It has lighting and color-correction commands, along with tools for fixing image defects, making selections, adding text, and painting on your images. You can rearrange the Standard Edit workspace to best suit your needs by moving, hiding, and showing palettes;

arranging palettes in the Palette Bin; zooming in or out of the photo; scrolling to a different area of the document window; and creating multiple windows and views.

The Standard Edit workspace has the following components:

Menu bar Contains menus for performing tasks. The menus are organized by topic. For example, the Enhance menu contains commands for applying adjustments to an image.

Shortcuts bar Displays buttons for implementing common commands, like Save 💾 and Print 🖨 .

Workspace buttons Moves you between the Quick Fix 🖼 and Standard Edit 🖼 workspaces.

Toolbox Holds tools for editing images.

Options bar Provides options for the tool you select.

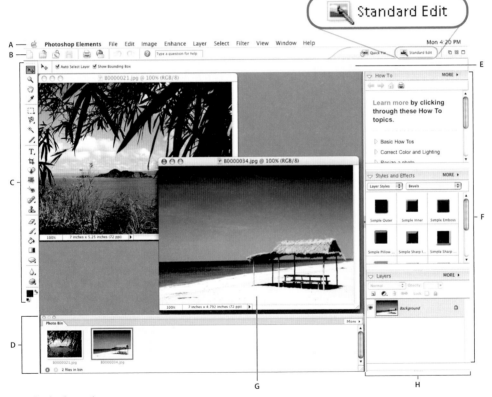

Standard Edit workspace
A. Menu bar B. Shortcuts bar C. Toolbox D. Photo bin E. Options bar F. Palettes G. Active image area
H. Palette bin

Palettes Help you monitor and modify images.

Palette Bin Helps you organize the palettes in your work area.

Photo Bin Displays thumbnails of open photos.

For more information, see "To correct color in Quick Fix" on page 67.

About the Quick Fix workspace

The Quick Fix workspace ⬚ contains simple tools and commands to quickly fix common problems. If you are new to digital imaging, Quick Fix is a good place to start fixing photos. It has many of the basic tools for correcting color and lighting. Most of the time, you can adjust a photo using adjustment sliders, which take the guess-work out of fixing red eyes, lighting, color problems, and sharpening.

The Quick Fix workspace has the following components:

Menu bar Contains menus for performing tasks. The menus are organized by topic. For example, the Enhance menu contains commands for applying adjustments to an image.

Shortcuts bar Displays buttons for implementing common commands, like Save 🖫 and Print 🖨 .

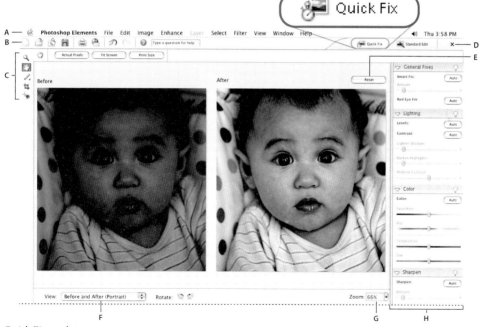

Quick Fix workspace
A. *Menu bar* ***B.*** *Shortcuts bar* ***C.*** *Tools* ***D.*** *Close image* ***E.*** *Reset the After image to be the same as the Before image* ***F.*** *View menu* ***G.*** *Zoom menu* ***H.*** *Fixing options*

Workspace buttons Moves you between the Quick Fix 🖼 and Standard Edit 🖼 workspaces.

Tools Holds the Zoom tool, Hand tool, Magic Selection Brush tool, Crop tool, and Red Eye Removal tool for editing images.

Adjustment sliders Provides sliders you drag to adjust the lighting, color, and sharpness of an image.

View menu Choose an option to display the photo you're fixing.

Photo Bin Displays thumbnails of open photos.

About the Bridge workspace

Adobe Bridge is tightly integrated with Photoshop Elements to help you view, find, manage, and organize your photos. It is optimized for quick access and retrieval of photos. You can use Bridge to view thumbnails of images without opening Photoshop Elements. For more information, see "The Bridge work area" on page 33.

To exit Photoshop Elements

1 Do one of the following:

• Choose File > Exit.

• Click the Close button in the top right corner of the workspace.

2 When closing the Editor, choose whether or not to save any open files.

How Tos, context menus, and shortcuts

To use the How To palette

In the Standard Edit workspace, the How To palette provides activities that guide you through different image-editing tasks. For example, you can view instructions about restoring an old photograph. Photoshop Elements will even do some of the steps for you.

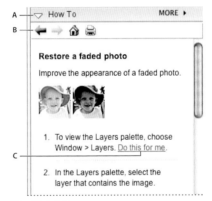

How To palette
A. Click the triangle to open or close the palette B. Navigation and Print buttons C. Click Do This For Me to have Photoshop Elements perform the task.

1 If necessary, open the How To palette by clicking its triangle ▷ in the Palette Bin. If the How To palette isn't visible in the Palette Bin or the work area, choose Window > How To.

The main menu of How To categories appears in the palette.

2 Click a How To category to view a list of How Tos, and then click the How To you want to use.

Note: You can use the navigation arrows ⬅ ➡ *to move between the How To's you view. A Home button* 🏠 *takes you back to the main menu.*

3 Follow the instructions in the How To. When available, you can click Do This For Me to have Photoshop Elements perform the task for you. If you want to print a set of instructions, click the Print button 🖨 .

To use context menus

Context-sensitive menus display commands that are relevant to the active tool, selection, or palette. Often times, these menus are another way to access commands from palettes.

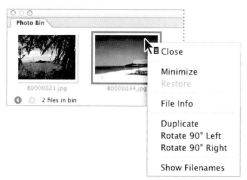

Control-click to open a context menu

1 Position the pointer over an image or palette item.

Note: *Not all palettes offer context menus.*

2 Control-click and choose a command from the menu that appears.

About the shortcuts bar

The shortcuts bar displays buttons for common commands. To see the name of a button, position the pointer over the button. Its tool tip appears.

Click the Help Contents button 🔘 in the shortcuts bar to open the Adobe Help Center, where you can search through Help topics to find the answers you need.

You can also use the search text box in the shortcuts bar to perform searches. Type a word or a phrase, press Return, and the Photoshop Elements Help window appears. You can click a link for more information about your search topic.

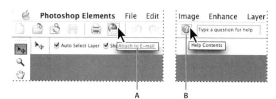

Tool tips in the Editor shortcuts bar
A. Click a hot tool tip to access more information in Adobe Help Center. *B. Click the Help Contents button to open Adobe Help Center.*

Using keyboard commands and modifier keys

Keyboard commands let you quickly execute commands without using a menu; modifier keys let you alter how a tool operates. When available, the keyboard command appears to the right of the command name in the menu.

🔘 *For a list of keyboard shortcuts, see the Keyboard shortcuts topic in Help.*

Tools

About the toolbox

You use tools in the toolbox to select, edit, and view images; some tools let you paint, draw, and type. The toolbox appears on the left side of the Standard Edit and Quick Fix workspaces. In the Standard Edit workspace, you can move the toolbox by dragging the gripper bar at the top of the box.

You must select a tool in the toolbox before you can use it. Once selected, the tool is highlighted in the toolbox, and optional settings for the tool appear in the options bar, which is located below the shortcuts bar at the top of the Editor workspace. Some tools in the toolbox have additional tools beneath them. These are called *hidden tools*. A small triangle at the lower right of the tool icon signals that there are hidden tools. When you select a tool, any additional hidden tools appear in the options bar.

Note: You cannot deselect a tool—once you select a tool, it remains selected until you select a different tool. For example, if you've selected the Lasso tool, and you want to click in your image without selecting anything, select the Hand tool.

You can view information about any tool in the toolbox by positioning the pointer over it. The name of the tool appears below the pointer—this is called the *tool tip*. You can click a link in some tool tips to see additional information about the tool.

To select a tool

❖ Do one of the following:

- Click a tool in the toolbox. If there is a small triangle at a tool's lower right corner, hold down the mouse button to view the hidden tools nested with the tool. Then click the tool you want to select.

- Click a tool in the toolbox. Any additional hidden tools appear in the options bar. Click the tool you want to select.

- Press the tool's keyboard shortcut. The keyboard shortcut is displayed in its tool tip. For example, you can select the Move tool by pressing the V key.

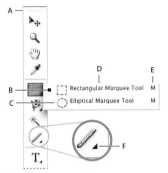

Using tools
A. Toolbox B. Active tool C. Hidden tools D. Tool name E. Tool shortcut F. Hidden tool triangle

To set tool preferences

1 In the Editor, choose Photoshop Elements > Preferences > General.

2 Set one or more of the following options:

- Select Show Tool Tips to show or hide tool tips.

- Select Use Shift Key For Tool Switch to cycle through a set of hidden tools by holding down the Shift key. When this option is deselected, you can

Toolbox overview

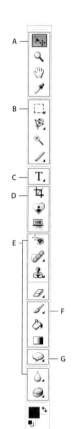

A

B

C
D

E

F

G

A Navigation and measuring tools

- ▸⊕ **Move (V)**
- ⚲ **Zoom (Z)**
- ✋ **Hand (H)**
- ⚲ **Eyedropper (I)**

B Selection tools

- ⬚ **Rectangular Marquee (M)**
  - ◯ Elliptical Marquee (M)
  - ◯ Lasso (L)
- ▨ **Magnetic Lasso (L)**
  - ▷ Polygonal Lasso (L)
- ⚲ **Magic Wand (W)**
- ⚲ **Magic Selection Brush (F)**
  - ⚲ Selection Brush (A)

C Type tools

- T **Horizontal Type (T)**
  - ⁞T Vertical Type (T)
  - T Horizontal Type Mask (T)
  - T Vertical Type Mask (T)

D Crop tools

- ⛏ **Crop (C)**
- ⚲ **Cookie Cutter (Q)**
- ▭ **Straighten (P)**

E Retouching tools

- ⚲ **Red Eye Removal (Y)**
- ⚲ **Spot Healing Brush (J)**
  - ⚲ Healing Brush (J)
- ⚲ **Clone Stamp (S)**
  - ⚲ Pattern Stamp (S)
- ⚲ **Eraser (E)**
  - ⚲ Background Eraser (E)
  - ⚲ Magic Eraser (E)
- ⚲ **Blur (R)**
  - △ Sharpen (R)
  - ⚲ Smudge (R)
- ⚲ **Sponge (O)**
  - ⚲ Dodge (O)
  - ⚲ Burn (O)

F Painting and drawing tools

- ⚲ **Brush (B)**
  - ⚲ Pencil (N)
  - ⚲ Impressionist Brush (B)
  - ⚲ Color Replacement (B)
- ⚲ **Paint Bucket (K)**
- ▨ **Gradient (G)**

G Shape tools

- ▭ Rectangle (U)
- ▭ Rounded Rectangle (U)
- ◯ Ellipse (U)
- ◯ Polygon (U)
- ╲ Line (U)
- ⚲ **Custom Shape (U)**
  - ▸ Shape Selection (U)

■ Indicates default tool   * Keyboard shortcuts appear in parenthesis

cycle through a set of hidden tools by pressing the shortcut key (without holding down Shift).

3 Click OK.

To set the appearance of a tool pointer

1 In the Editor, choose Photoshop Elements > Preferences > Display & Cursors.

2 Select a setting for the Painting Cursors:

Standard Displays pointers as tool icons.

Precise Displays pointers as crosshairs.

Normal Brush Tip Displays the pointers as circles at 50% of the size you specify for the brush.

Full Size Brush Tip Displays the pointers as circles at the full size you specify for the brush.

Show Crosshair in Brush Tip Displays crosshairs in the circles when you choose either Normal Brush Tip or Full Size Brush Tip.

3 Select a setting for Other Cursors:

Standard Displays pointers as tool icons.

Precise Displays pointers as crosshairs.

To set tool options

The options bar appears below the shortcuts bar at the top of the Editor workspace. The options bar is context sensitive—it changes as you select different tools. Some settings in the options bar are common to several tools, and some are specific to one tool.

Lasso options bar
A. *Tool icon* **B.** *Active tool* **C.** *Hidden tools* **D.** *Tool options*

1 Select a tool.

2 Look in the options bar to see the available options. For more information on setting options for a specific tool, search for the tool's name in Photoshop Elements Help.

Note: *To return a tool or all tools to their default settings, click the tool icon in the options bar, then choose Reset Tool or Reset All Tools from the context menu.*

To set a completed operations alert

1 In the Editor, choose Photoshop Elements > Preferences > General.

2 Select Beep When Done, and click OK.

Palettes and bins

About palettes

Palettes help you manage, monitor, and modify images. Some palettes have menus that provide additional commands and options. You can organize palettes in the workspace in many different ways. You can store palettes in the Palette Bin to keep them out of your way but easily accessible, or you can keep frequently used palettes open in the workspace. Another option is to group palettes together or dock one palette at the bottom of another palette.

Note: Drag a palette out of the Palette Bin if you want to remove it from the Palette Bin and keep it open.

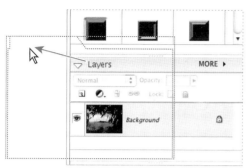

Dragging a palette

Palette menus

Some commands appear in both the palette menu and the menu bar. Other commands are exclusive to palette menus.

Only those palettes with a More button at the top have a menu. Click More to choose a command from the palette menu. The location and appearance of the More button depend on whether the palette is located in the Palette Bin or in a palette group.

Pop-up sliders within palettes

Some palettes and dialog boxes contain settings that use pop-up sliders (for example, the Opacity option in the Layers palette). If there is a triangle next to the text box, you can activate the pop-up slider by clicking the triangle. Position the pointer over the triangle next to the setting, hold down the mouse button, and drag the slider or angle radius to the desired value. Click outside the slider box or press to close the slider box. To cancel changes, press Esc.

To increase or decrease values in 10% increments when the pop-up slider box is open, hold down Shift and press the Up Arrow or Down Arrow key.

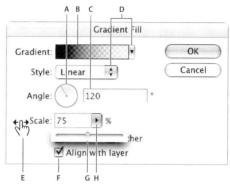

Different ways to enter values
A. Dial B. Click to open window C. Text box D. Menu arrow
E. Scrubby slider F. Check box G. Slider H. Pop-up slider triangle

To work with palettes in the Editor

The Palette Bin in Standard Edit lets you store multiple palettes in a single area that you can easily configure, close, or keep open for easy and fast access. By default, the Palette Bin appears on the right side of the workspace.

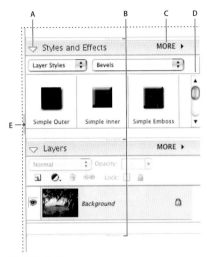

The Palette Bin
A. *Collapse or expand palette* **B.** *Dotted-line bar, drag up or down to adjust palette height* **C.** *Palette menu* **D.** *Scroll to view rest of palette* **E.** *Dark gray bar, click to show or hide Palette Bin or drag left or right to adjust palette width*

1 To adjust the Palette Bin, do any of the following:

• To adjust its width and height, drag the dark gray bar on the left side or dotted-line bar on the bottom.

• To show or hide the bin, choose Window > Palette Bin, or click the dark gray bar on the Palette Bin's left edge to hide it or on the right side of the Editor window to show it.

2 To use palettes in the Palette Bin, do any of the following:

• To remove a palette from the Palette Bin, drag the palette's title bar out of the Palette Bin.

• To add a palette to the Palette Bin, drag the palette's title bar into the Palette Bin. Or, click the More button in the palette and select Place In Palette Bin When Closed; then close the palette.

• To rearrange palettes in the Palette Bin, drag the palette's title bar to a new location.

• To expand or collapse palettes in the Palette Bin, click the triangle next to the palette's name.

3 To use palettes outside of the Palette Bin, do any of the following:

• To open a palette, choose the palette's name in the Window menu.

• To close a palette, choose the palette's name in the Window menu. Or click the Close button in the palette's tab.

• To change the size of a palette, drag the gripper corner of the palette.

• To show or hide all open palettes, press Tab.

• To group palettes together, drag another palette's tab onto the body of the target palette. A thick line appears around the body of the target palette when the pointer is over the correct area for grouping to occur. If you want to move a palette to another group, drag the palette's tab to that group. To separate a palette from a group, drag the palette's tab outside the group.

• To move a palette group, drag the title bar.

• To expand or collapse a palette or palette group, double-click the palette's tab or title bar, or click the green resize button in the upper left corner of the title bar.

• To dock palettes together, drag a palette's tab (not title bar) to the bottom of another palette. A double line appears at the bottom of the target palette when the pointer is over the correct area. You cannot dock entire palette groups together.

• To reset palettes to their default positions, choose Window > Reset Palette Locations.

Note: If you want palettes to always open in their default positions in the Editor, choose Photoshop Elements > Preferences > General, and then deselect Save Palette Locations. The change takes effect the next time you start the application.

To use the Photo Bin in the Editor

Located at the bottom of the Standard Edit and Quick Fix workspaces, the Photo Bin displays thumbnails of open photos. It's useful for switching between photos in your workspace, especially if you have multiple images open. The Photo Bin has controls that let you open or close images, hide images, navigate through open images, make a specific image the frontmost, duplicate an image, rotate an image, or view file information. Since the Photo Bin appears in both Standard Edit and Quick Fix, you can easily bring open images into Quick Fix for edits.

❖ Do any of the following:

• To open an image in Photoshop Elements, drag a file from any location on your computer or from any storage device connected to your computer into the Photo Bin.

Note: The number of open files is displayed next to the Navigation buttons.

• To bring an opened image forward as the frontmost image, either click a thumbnail or use the Navigation buttons to select a thumbnail.

• Drag thumbnails to reorder them in the Photo Bin.

• To close an image, right-click a thumbnail in the Photo Bin and choose Close.

• To hide an image, right-click the thumbnail and choose Minimize from the context menu.

Note: To show an image after hiding it, either click the thumbnail in the Photo Bin, or right-click the thumbnail and choose Restore from the context menu.

• To view a photo's file information, right-click a thumbnail and choose File Info from the context menu.

• To duplicate an image, Option-click a thumbnail and choose Duplicate from the context menu. Photoshop Elements asks you to give the duplicate file a name.

• To rotate an image, right-click a thumbnail and choose Rotate 90• Left or Rotate 90• Right from the context menu.

• To show file names, right-click in the Photo Bin and choose Show Filenames from the context menu.

• To open or close the Photo Bin, choose Window > Photo Bin.

Viewing images in the Editor

Viewing images in Standard Edit or Quick Fix

In Standard Edit or Quick Fix, the Hand tool ✋ , the zoom tools ⊕ ⊖ , the zoom commands, and the Navigator palette let you view different areas of an image at different magnifications. The document window is where your image appears. You can open additional windows to display several views of an image at once (such as different magnifications).

You can magnify or reduce your view using various methods. The window's title bar displays the zoom percentage (unless the window is too small for the display to fit).

If you want to view another area of an image, either use the window scroll bars or select the Hand tool and drag to pan over the image. You can also use the Navigator palette.

💡 *To use the Hand tool while another tool is selected, hold down the spacebar as you drag in the image.*

Dragging the Hand tool to view another area of an image

To zoom in or out

❖ In Standard Edit or Quick Fix, do one of the following:

- Select a zoom tool 🔍, and click either the Zoom In ⊕ or Zoom Out ⊖ button in the options bar. Click the area you want to magnify. Each click magnifies or reduces the image to the next preset

percentage, and centers the display around the point you click. When the image has reached its maximum magnification level of 1600% or minimum reduction level of 1%, the magnifying glass appears empty.

Note: You can drag a zoom tool over the part of an image you want to magnify. Make sure that the Zoom In button is selected in the options bar. To move the zoom marquee around the image, begin dragging a marquee and then hold down the spacebar while dragging the marquee to a new location.

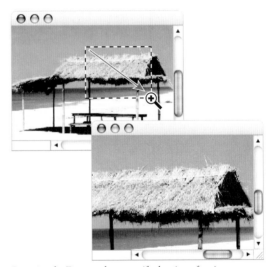

Dragging the Zoom tool to magnify the view of an image

- Click the Zoom In ⊕ or Zoom Out ⊖ button in the Navigator palette.

- Choose View > Zoom In or View > Zoom Out.

- (Quick Fix) Drag the Zoom slider, located below the image in the work area.

- Enter the desired magnification level in the Zoom text box either in the status bar or in the Navigator palette.

 When using a zoom tool, hold down Option to switch between zooming in and zooming out.

To display an image at 100%

❖ In Standard Edit or Quick Fix, do one of the following:

- Double-click the Zoom tool 🔍 in the toolbox.

- Select a zoom tool or the Hand tool, and click Actual Pixels in the options bar.

- Choose View > Actual Pixels, or Control-click the image and choose Actual Pixels.

- Enter 100% in the zoom box (at the lower-left corner of the image window) and press Return.

To speed up previews

You can speed up an image preview by temporarily doubling the size of the pixels, thus halving the resolution of the preview. This option has no effect on the pixels in the file; it simply provides faster previews.

1 In the Editor, choose Photoshop Elements > Preferences > Display & Cursors.

2 Select Use Pixel Doubling, and click OK.

To fit an image to the screen

❖ In Standard Edit or Quick Fix, do one of the following:

- Double-click the Hand tool 🖑 in the toolbox.

- Select a zoom tool or the Hand tool, and click the Fit Screen button in the options bar, or Control-click and choose Fit On Screen.

- Choose View > Fit On Screen.

These options scale both the zoom level and the window size to fit the available screen space.

To resize the window while zooming

❖ With a zoom tool active, select Resize Windows To Fit in the options bar. The window changes size as you magnify or reduce the view of the image.

When Resize Windows To Fit is deselected, the window maintains a constant size regardless of the image's magnification. This can be helpful when you are using smaller monitors or working with tiled images.

Note: *To automatically resize the window when using keyboard shortcuts to reduce or magnify an image view, in the Editor choose Photoshop Elements > Preferences > General, and then select the Zoom Resizes Windows preference and click OK.*

Using the Navigator palette

The Navigator palette lets you adjust the image's magnification and area of view. Typing a value in the text box, clicking the Zoom Out or Zoom In button, or dragging the zoom slider changes the magnification. Drag the view box in the image thumbnail to move the view of an image. The view box represents the boundaries of the image window. You can also click in the thumbnail of the image to designate the area of view.

Note: To change the color of the view box, choose Palette Options from the Navigator palette menu. Choose a color from the Color menu or click the color swatch to open the Color Picker and select a custom color. Click OK.

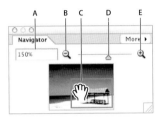

The Navigator palette
A. Zoom text box B. Zoom Out C. Drag the view box to move the view D. Zoom slider E. Zoom In

To open multiple windows of the same image

In the Standard Edit workspace, you can open multiple windows to display different views of the same file. A list of open windows appears in the Window menu, and thumbnails of each open image appear in the Photo Bin. Available memory may limit the number of windows per image.

❖ Choose View > New Window For *[image file name]*. Depending on the position of the first window, you may have to move the second window to view both simultaneously.

💡 *You can use the New Window command when you're working with a zoomed image to see what the image will look like at 100% size in a separate window.*

To view and arrange multiple windows

❖ In Standard Edit, do one of the following:

• To display windows stacked and cascading from the upper left to the lower right of the screen, choose Window > Images > Cascade. You can also click the Automatically Cascade Windows button 🗗 in the upper right portion of the work area.

• To display windows edge to edge, choose Window > Images > Tile. You can also click the Automatically Tile Windows button 🔳 in the upper right portion of the work area. As you close images, the open windows are resized to fill the available space.

• To view all open images at the same magnification as the active image, choose Window > Images > Match Zoom.

• To view the same section (upper left corner, center, lower right corner, and so on) of all open photos, choose Window > Images > Match Location. The view in all windows shifts to match the active (frontmost) image. The zoom level does not change.

To close windows

❖ In Standard Edit, do one of the following:

• Choose File > Close to close the active window.

• Click the Close button on the title bar of the active window.

• Control-click a thumbnail in the Photo Bin and choose Close.

• Choose File > Close All to close all open windows.

Undo, redo, and cancel

To undo, redo or cancel operations

Many operations can be undone or redone again. For instance, you can restore all or part of an image to its last saved version. Available memory may limit your ability to use these options.

1 To undo or redo an operation, do one of the following:

• Choose Edit > Undo or choose Edit > Redo.

• Click the Undo button 🔄 or the Redo button 🔄 in the shortcuts bar.

Note: If an operation can't be undone, the command dims.

2 To cancel an operation, hold down Command and the period key until the operation in progress stops.

Using the Undo History palette (Editor only)

The Undo History palette (Window > Undo History) lets you jump to any recent state of the image created during the current work session. Each time you apply a change to pixels in an image, the new state of that image is added to the Undo History palette.

For example, if you select, paint, and rotate part of an image, each of those states is listed separately in the palette. You can then select any of the states, and the image reverts to how it looked when that change was first applied. You can then work from that state.

Actions, such as zooming and scrolling, do not affect pixels in the image and do not appear in the Undo History palette. Nor do program-wide changes, such as changes to palettes, color settings, and preferences.

The Undo History palette
A. Original state B. State C. Selected state and state slider

Note the following guidelines when using the Undo History palette:

• By default, the Undo History palette lists 50 previous states. Older states are automatically deleted to free more memory for Photoshop Elements. You can change the number of states displayed in the Undo History palette in General Preferences. The maximum number of states is 1000.

• The original state of the photo is always displayed at the top of the Undo History palette. You can always revert an image to its original state by clicking this top state. Clicking the original state is also handy for comparing before and after versions of your editing.

• When you close and reopen the document, all states from the last working session are cleared from the palette.

• States are added to the bottom of the list. That is, the oldest state is at the top of the list, the most recent one at the bottom.

• Each state is listed with the name of the tool or command used to change the image.

• Selecting a state dims those below. This way you can easily see which changes will be discarded if you continue working from the selected state.

- Selecting a state and then changing the image eliminates all states that came after it. Likewise, deleting a state deletes that state and those that came after it.

To revert to the last saved version

When editing a photo in Standard Edit or Quick Fix, you can revert to the last saved version.

❖ Choose Edit > Revert.

Note: Revert is added as a history state in the Undo History palette and can be undone.

To revert to a previous state of an image

❖ In Standard Edit or Quick Fix, do any of the following:

- Click the name of the state in the Undo History palette.

- Drag the slider at the left of the state up or down to a different state in the Undo History palette.

- Click the Undo ↺ or Redo ↻ buttons on the shortcuts bar.

- Choose Undo or Redo from the Undo History palette menu or the Edit menu.

💡 *To set the keyboard command for Step Forward and Step Backward, choose Photoshop Elements > Preferences > General, and choose from the Step Back/Fwd menu.*

To delete one or more states from the Undo History palette

❖ Do one of the following:

- To delete a state, click the name of the state, and choose Delete from the Undo History palette menu. States following the one you selected are also deleted.

- To delete the list of states from the Undo History palette, without changing the image, choose Clear Undo History from the palette menu or choose Edit > Clear > Undo History. Clearing is useful for freeing up memory, especially if you get an alert that Photoshop Elements is low on memory.

Note: Clearing the Undo History palette cannot be undone.

To clear memory used by the clipboard and the Undo History palette

You can delete items copied to the clipboard or states in the Undo History palette to free up memory.

❖ In Standard Edit, do one of the following:

- To clear memory used by the clipboard, choose Edit > Clear > Clipboard Contents.

- To clear memory used by the Undo History palette, choose Edit > Clear > Undo History or choose Clear Undo History from the Undo History palette menu.

- To clear the memory used in both the clipboard and the Undo History palette simultaneously, choose Edit > Clear > All.

Note: Clearing the Undo History palette or clipboard cannot be undone.

Presets and libraries (Editor only)

To use preset tool options

In the Standard Edit workspace, pop-up palettes appear in the options bar and provide access to predefined libraries of brushes, color swatches, gradients, patterns, layer styles, and custom shapes. The items in each library are called *presets*. When closed, pop-up palettes display a thumbnail image of the currently selected preset.

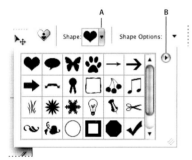

Viewing the Cookie Cutter pop-up palette in the options bar
***A.** Click to show the pop-up palette.* ***B.** Click to view the pop-up palette menu, which contains preset libraries.*

You can change the display of a pop-up palette to view presets by their names, as thumbnail icons, or with both names and icons.

You can use the Presets Manager to load different preset libraries. Presets are stored in separate library files that can be found in the Presets folder in the Photoshop Elements application folder.

1 Select the tool you want to use.

2 In the options bar, open the pop-up palette. Only certain tools have a pop-up palette in the options bar.

3 Do any of the following:

• To view and select currently loaded preset libraries, click the triangle in the upper right corner of the pop-up palette.

• To select a preset, click an item in the library.

• To save a brush, open the pop-up palette menu, choose the Save Brush command, then enter a name in the dialog box provided and click OK.

• To save a gradient or pattern, open the pop-up palette menu, choose the New Gradient or New Pattern command, then enter a name in the dialog box provided and click OK.

• To rename a brush, gradient, or pattern in a pop-up palette, open the pop-up palette menu, choose the Rename command, then enter a new name and click OK.

• To delete a brush, gradient, or pattern from a pop-up palette, select an item, open the pop-up palette menu and choose the Delete command. You can also Hold down Option and click a brush or gradient.

• To save a library of brushes, gradients, or patterns, open the pop-up palette menu. From the menu, choose the Save Brushes, Save Gradients, or Save Patterns command, then enter a name for the library file, and click Save.

• To load a library of brushes, gradients, or patterns, open the pop-up palette menu, choose the Load command, then select the library file you want to add and click Load.

Note: Using the Load command adds the brush library to the brushes you have available. If you choose a preset library of brushes, the preset library replaces your current set of brushes.

• To replace the current set of gradients in a pop-up palette, open the pop-up palette menu, choose a library file from the bottom section of the palette menu, and click OK. You can also choose the Replace command, browse to select a library file, and click Load.

• To replace the current set of brushes or patterns in a pop-up palette, choose a library from the Brushes menu.

Note: To replace the current set of brushes, gradients, or patterns, you can also choose Preset Manager from the pop-up palette menu and use the Preset Manager to load a different library of brushes, gradients, or patterns.

• To load the default set of brushes, gradients, or patterns, open the pop-up palette menu and choose the Reset command.

For more information about using presets, search for presets in Help.

About the Preset Manager

In the Standard Edit workspace, the Preset Manager (Edit > Preset Manager) lets you manage the libraries of preset brushes, color swatches, gradients, and patterns that come with Photoshop Elements. For example, you can create a set of favorite brushes, or you can restore the default presets.

Each type of library is a file with its own file extension and default folder. Preset files are installed on your computer inside the Presets folder in the Photoshop Elements program folder.

Note: You can delete a preset in the Preset Manager by selecting the preset and clicking Delete. You can always use the Reset command to restore the default items in a library.

Dragging a preset to a new position in the Preset Manager

For more information on using preset libraries, search for library in Help.

Chapter 4: Using Adobe Bridge

The basics of Bridge

About Adobe Bridge

Adobe Bridge is a cross-platform application provided with Photoshop Elements for Mac OS, Adobe Creative Suite 2, and Adobe Production Studio. You can use Bridge to organize, browse, and locate files. You can create new folders; rename, move, and delete files; edit metadata; rotate images; and run batch commands. You can also view information about files and data imported from your digital or DV camera.

The Bridge work area

The main components of the Adobe Bridge window are as follows:

Look In menu Lists the folder hierarchy, as well as favorite and recent folders. Use this menu to quickly find folders and files you want to display. The menu is at the top of the Bridge window.

Favorites panel Provides quick access to folders.

Note: If you have Adobe Creative Suite 2, you also have access to Version Cue and Bridge Center. For more information about these features, see Help in a Creative Suite application, such as Illustrator.

Folders panel Shows the folder hierarchy on your computer. Use this panel to navigate to folders.

Preview panel Displays a preview of the selected file. The preview is separate from, and typically larger than, the thumbnail image displayed in the content area. You can reduce or enlarge the preview.

Metadata panel Contains metadata information for the selected file. If multiple files are selected, shared data (such as keywords, date created, and exposure setting) is listed.

Keywords panel Helps you organize your images by attaching keywords to them.

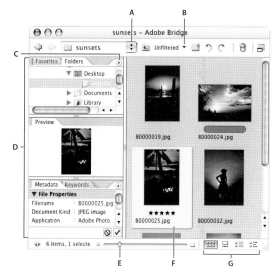

Adobe Bridge
A. *Look In menu* **B.** *Menu for sorting by rating or label* **C.** *Panel menu* **D.** *Panels* **E.** *Thumbnail slider for zooming* **F.** *Selected thumbnail* **G.** *View options*

To start and quit Bridge

Do any of the following:

• To open Bridge from Photoshop Elements, click the Browse with Bridge icon 🔲 or choose File > Browse With Bridge.

- To open Bridge directly, double-click the Adobe Bridge icon 🖌. By default, this icon is located in the Applications/Adobe Bridge folder.

- To quit Bridge, choose Bridge > Quit Bridge.

- To return to the last open application that started Bridge, choose File > Return To *[Application]*.

💡 *If you install an Adobe Creative Suite application or an Adobe Production Studio application, Bridge offers additional features. For more information, see the application's Help.*

For more information, see "To organize files and folders with Bridge" on page 36.

To create and close Bridge windows

❖ Do one of the following:

- Choose File > New Window to create a full-size Bridge window.

- Choose File > Close Window.

For more information, see "The Bridge work area" on page 33.

To use Bridge in Compact mode

Switch to Compact mode when you want to shrink the Bridge window. In Compact mode, the panels are hidden and the content area is simplified. A subset of common Bridge commands remains available from the pop-up menu at the upper right portion of the window.

By default, the Compact mode Bridge window floats on top of all windows. (In Full mode, the Bridge window can move behind application windows.) This floating window is useful because it is always visible

and usable as you work in different applications. For instance, you might use Compact mode after you select the files you plan to use, and then drag them into the application as needed.

1 Click the Switch To Compact Mode button 🗗.

2 Do any of the following:

- Choose commands from the menu at the top right of the Bridge window.

- Click the Switch To Ultra Compact Mode button ▭ to hide the content area, further minimizing the Bridge window. You can click the button again to return to Compact mode.

- Click the Switch To Full Mode button 🖳 to return to Full mode, displaying the content area and the panels, and letting Bridge move behind the current application window.

To adjust the Bridge window

You can customize the Bridge window by moving and resizing the panels. For example, you can enlarge the Preview panel to display bigger thumbnails. However, you can't move panels outside the Bridge window.

❖ Do any of the following:

- Drag a panel by its tab up or down into another panel area.

- Drag the horizontal divider bar between panels to make them larger or smaller.

- Drag the vertical divider bar between the panels and the content area right or left to resize the panels or content area.

- Click the Show/Hide Panes button ◀▶ at the lower left of the Bridge window to display or hide the panels.

- Choose View, followed by the name of the panel you want to display or hide.

Files and folders in Bridge

To view file and folder thumbnails in Bridge

The content area of Bridge displays thumbnails of the files and folders of the selected folder, along with information about them. You can specify how you want files and folders to be displayed in the content area.

❖ Do any of the following:

- Drag the Thumbnail slider △ at the bottom of the Bridge window to adjust the size of thumbnails.

- Choose View > As Thumbnails to display items in a grid.

- Choose View > As Filmstrip to display thumbnails in a scrolling list along with an extra-large thumbnail of the currently selected item. Click the Back button or Forward button directly below the extra-large thumbnail to go to the previous or next thumbnail. Click the Switch Filmstrip Orientation button ⌗ to change from a horizontal slide show to a vertical one. Note that you can page through a PDF preview in Filmstrip view.

- Choose View > As Details to display a scrollable list of thumbnails along with information about the selected file.

- Choose View > Show Thumbnail Only to view thumbnails without any text information listed.

- Choose View > Slide Show to view thumbnails as a slide show that takes over the entire screen. This is a quick and easy way to display and work with large versions of all the graphics files in a folder. Instructions on how to use the slide show are displayed on the screen when you choose this command.

To specify how files and folders are shown in Bridge

You can specify what type of files and folders you want to display as thumbnails in the content area, as well as the order in which to display them.

❖ Choose any of the following commands from the View menu:

- Sort, followed by the order in which you want to sort files. Choose Ascending to sort in ascending rather than descending order. Choose Manually to sort by the last order in which you dragged the files.

- Show Hidden Files to display hidden files, such as cache files.

- Show Folders to display folders as well as individual files.

- Show All Files to display all files regardless of type, even non-Adobe files that Bridge doesn't normally display.

- Show Graphic Files Only to display only files in graphic file formats, such as Camera Raw, EPS, JPEG, BMP, PS, TIFF, and GIF.

- Show Vector Files Only to display only files created with drawing programs such as Adobe Illustrator, and EPS and PS files.

- Refresh (or choose Refresh from the Folders panel menu) to update the content area. Closing and reopening Bridge also refreshes the view.

You can also click Unfiltered at the top right of the Bridge window and choose the files you want to display based on their rating or label. The Unfiltered menu operates independently of the View > Sort commands.

To navigate folders and files with Bridge

❖ Do any of the following:

- Select the Folders panel and click to select the folder you want. Click the triangle next to a folder or double-click the folder to open subfolders within it.

- Select the Favorites panel and click to select the folder you want.

- Choose a folder from the Look In menu. You can click the Go Back button, Go Forward button, or Go Up button next to the menu to navigate within the current folder listed in the menu.

For more information, see "To specify how files and folders are shown in Bridge" on page 35.

To select files in Bridge

Before you can work with a file, you need to select it. You can select more than one file at a time.

❖ Do one of the following in the current folder:

- Click the thumbnail of a file.

- To select contiguous files, Shift-click them.

- To select noncontiguous files, Command-click each file.

- To select all visible files, choose Edit > Select All.

- To select all labeled or unlabeled files, choose Edit > Select Labeled or Edit > Select Unlabeled.

- To select the opposite of the current selection, choose Edit > Invert Selection.

To open files in Bridge

You can open files in Bridge, even files that were not made with Adobe applications. If certain file types are not opening properly, check the File Type Associations settings in Preferences. (See To set Bridge preferences in Help.)

1 Select the file in the current folder.

2 Do one of the following:

- Choose File > Open.

- Press Return.

- Double-click the file in the content area or Preview panel.

- Choose File > Open With > Photoshop Elements 4.0.

- Drag the file into the working area of an application, such as an open Illustrator document.

- Drag the file onto the application icon.

If you choose File > Browse to launch Bridge within a Production Studio application, double-clicking a file opens or imports that file within the application.

To organize files and folders with Bridge

Adobe Bridge makes it easy to move files between folders, copy and duplicate them, and otherwise manipulate them.

💡 *Drag a folder onto the Preview panel to display its contents in Bridge.*

❖ Do any of the following:

To delete files Select the files and click the Delete button 🗑 or press Delete.

To copy files and folders Select the files or folders and choose Option-drag the file or folders to a different folder.

To move files to another folder Select the files and drag them to a different folder.

💡 *To quickly attach an image to an e-mail message, drag the image from Bridge and drop it into the e-mail message.*

To display the location of a file in the operating system Select the file and choose File > Reveal In Finder.

To find the location of a file in a collection Select a file and choose File > Reveal In Bridge. A collection is a saved search. By default, if you select a file in a collection, the file is listed as being located in the folder "File Results." Selecting Reveal In Bridge moves you to the folder in which the file is located.

To place files into an application Select the files and choose File > Place, followed by the name of the application. For instance, you can use this command to place a JPEG image into Illustrator. You can also drag files from Bridge into an application. Depending on the file, the document into which you want to place it may need to be opened first.

To drag files out of Bridge Select the files and drag them onto the desktop or into another folder. This action moves the file onto the desktop or folder.

To drag files into Bridge Select one or more files on the desktop, in a folder, or in another application that supports drag and drop, and drag them into the content area in Bridge. The files are moved from their current folder into the one displayed in Bridge. (If the file you are dragging is in a different mounted volume than Bridge, the file is copied into Bridge.)

To create new folders Choose File > New Folder. Then, enter a name when the folder appears in the content area.

To delete folders Select the folder and press Delete.

To add folders to Favorites Choose a folder from the Look In menu or Folders panel or select it in the content area. Then choose File > Add To Favorites. You can also drag the folder from the content area to the Favorites panel.

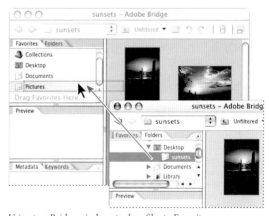

Using two Bridge windows to drag files to Favorites

To remove folders from Favorites In the Favorites panel, select the folder you want to remove. Then choose File > Remove From Favorites.

To reorganize folders in the Favorites panel Drag the folder to the desired location in the panel.

Note: If you have Adobe Creative Suite 2, you can also use Adobe Version Cue from Bridge to manage files you author. You can create and manage revisions to files kept in Version Cue projects. For more information, see Help in a Creative Suite application.

To apply keywords to files with Bridge

The Keyword panel lets you create and apply Bridge keywords to files. Keywords can be organized into categories called *keyword sets*. Using keywords, you identify files based on their content. Later, you can view all files with shared keywords as a group.

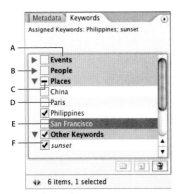

Keywords panel
A. Keyword set B. Click to show/hide content of keyword set
C. Set with one or more keywords applied D. Keyword E. Selected keyword F. Keyword applied

❖ Do any of the following:

• To add a keyword to files, select one or more files. In the Keywords panel, click the box next to the name of the keyword you want to add. A check mark appears in the box next to the keyword when it's added to a file.

• To add a set of keywords to files, select one or more files. In the Keywords panel, click the box next to the name of the keyword set. A check mark appears in the box next to the keyword set when it's added to a file.

💡 *Create a group of frequently used keywords so that you can apply them as a group.*

• To remove keywords from a file, select the file, and then click the box next to the name of the keyword or keyword set that you want to remove.

• To create a new keyword, click the New Keyword button 🔳 at the bottom of the panel or choose New Keyword from the panel menu. A new default keyword name appears in the panel. To create the new keyword, type over the default name and press Return.

• To create a new keyword set, click the New Keyword Set button 🔳 at the bottom of the panel or choose New Keyword Set from the panel menu. A new default keyword set name appears in the panel. To create the new keyword set, type over the default name and press Return.

• To rename a keyword or keyword set, select the keyword or keyword set and choose Rename from the panel menu. Then, type over the name in the panel and press Return.

Note: When you rename a keyword, the keyword's name isn't changed in files that currently contain it. The original name stays in the file.

• To move a keyword to a different keyword set, drag the keyword from one set to another.

• To delete a keyword, select the keyword by clicking its name, and then click the Delete Keyword button 🗑 at the bottom of the panel or choose Delete from the panel menu.

Note: Keywords that you get from other users appear in the Other Keywords category until you recategorize them. To make these keywords permanent in Bridge, select the keyword and then choose Persistent from the context menu.

• To find a file using the keyword, choose Find from the panel menu.

To label files with Bridge

Labeling files with a certain color is a flexible way to mark a large number of files quickly. Using the View > Sort menu or Unfilter button, you can choose to view files according to their color label.

For example, suppose you've just imported a large number of images and are viewing them in Bridge. As you review each new image, you can label those you want to keep. After this initial pass, you can use the Unfilter button to display and work on files that you've labeled with a particular color.

You can assign names to labels through the Preferences dialog box. (See To set Bridge preferences in Help.) The name is then added to the file's metadata when you apply the label.

To search for labeled images, you must select Label from the first pop-up menu, and then type in the label name, Red for example. Then all files labeled Red will be found.

Note: When you view folders, Bridge shows both labeled and unlabeled files until you choose another option. Also, purging the cache deletes labels from files that don't support XMP write (such as Camera Raw, BMP, DCS, Pict, PS6 PDF, and PSB files), locked files, or read-only files (such as files on CDs).

1 Select one or more files.

2 Do one of the following:

• To label files, choose a color from the Label menu.

• To remove labels from files, choose Label > No Label.

To rate files with Bridge

When assigning ratings to files, you can award from zero to five stars. Using the View > Sort menu or Unfilter button, you can choose to view files according to their rating.

For example, suppose you've just imported a large number of images and are viewing them in Bridge. As you review each new image, you can rate them from best to worst. After this initial pass, you can view only files you've rated with four or five stars and work on those.

1 Select one or more files.

2 Do any of the following:

• In Thumbnail view, click the dot representing the number of stars you want to give the file. (Dots do not appear in very small thumbnail views. If necessary, rescale the thumbnail view until the dots appear.)

• Choose a rating from the Label menu.

- To add or remove one star, choose Label > Increase Rating or Label > Decrease Rating.

- To remove all stars, choose Label > No Rating.

To search for files and folders with Bridge

You can perform searches with Bridge. You can narrow your search by adding multiple search criteria. You can even save your search criteria as a *collection*, so that you can perform the same search again later.

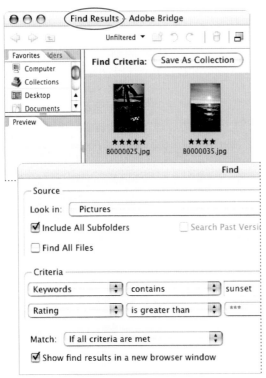

Search criteria, and results from the search

1 Choose Edit > Find.

2 In the Find dialog box, choose a source folder from the Look In menu. By default, the menu displays the currently active folder. Click the Browse button to navigate to another folder.

3 (Optional) Select Include All Subfolders to expand the search to any subfolders in the source folder.

4 (Optional) Select Show Find Results In A New Browser Window to display the search results in a new Bridge window. If left unselected, the search results appear in the content area of the current window.

5 Choose a criterion for your search by selecting an option from the leftmost Criteria menu.

6 Select a limiter from the center Criteria menu.

7 Enter the search text in the text box at the right, if needed. You can enter basic search terms such as AND, OR, and * (for wild cards).

8 To add search criteria, click the plus sign button. To remove search criteria, click the minus sign button.

9 Click Find. Bridge displays the files that match the search criteria, and you can navigate through the files.

10 (Optional) To save the search criteria to perform the same search again, click Save As Collection. Enter a name for the collection. Select Start Search From Current Folder to search from the same folder in the future. Then, click Save. The search criteria are saved in the Collections folder listed in the Favorites panel.

Chapter 5: Opening and saving files

Acquiring image files

To acquire and open images from digital cameras

❖ Do one of the following:

- Click the Connect To Camera or Scanner button in the Welcome window, and then choose the digital camera name from the Import menu in the Select Import Source dialog box.

- Choose File > Import, and select your digital camera from the submenu.

- From the Welcome Screen, click Import Photos From Camera.

If you're not able to acquire photos automatically, simply download your photos to a destination folder, and then open the images.

Opening files

To open a file

You can open and import images in various file formats in Standard Edit and Quick Fix. The available formats appear in the Open dialog box, the Open As dialog box, and the Import submenu.

1 Choose File > Open.

2 Locate and select the file you want to open. If the file does not appear, choose All Readable Documents from the Enable menu in the Open dialog box.

3 Click Open. In some cases, a dialog box appears, letting you set format-specific options.

There may be instances when Photoshop Elements cannot determine the correct format for a file. For example, transferring a file between Mac OS˙ and Windows can cause the format to be mislabeled. In such cases, you must specify the correct format in which to open the file.

For information about supported file formats, opening recently used files, and opening different types of files, see Help.

For more information, see "To save changes to the current file" on page 43.

To open a photo from Bridge

1 In Bridge, select the file in the current folder.

2 Do one of the following:

- Choose File > Open.

- Press Return.

- Double-click the file in the content area or Preview panel.

- Choose File > Open With Photoshop Elements.

- Drag the file onto the application icon.

To open a PDF file

Portable Document Format (PDF) is a versatile file format that can represent both vector and bitmap data and can contain electronic document search and navigation features. PDF is the primary format for Adobe Acrobat.

With the Import PDF dialog box, you can preview the pages and images in a multipage PDF file, then decide if you want to open them. You can choose to import full pages (including text and graphics), or you can import just the images from a PDF file. If you import only the images, the resolution, size, and color mode of the images remains unchanged. If you import pages, you can change the resolution and color mode.

Each page is shown as a thumbnail. To increase the size, choose an option from the Thumbnail Size menu.

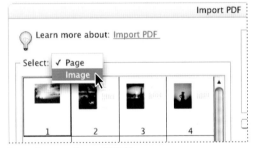

Importing pages from a PDF file

1 In Standard Edit, choose File > Open.

2 Select the name of the file, and click Open. You can change which types of files are shown by selecting an option from the Files of Type menu.

3 To import just the images from a PDF file, choose Image from the Select menu in the Import PDF dialog box. Select the image or images you want to open. (To select multiple images, Command-click each image.)

4 To import pages from a PDF file, choose Page from the Select menu, and then do any of the following:

- If the file contains multiple pages, select the page or pages you want to open, and click OK. (To select multiple pages, Command-click each page.)

- Under Page Options, accept the existing name, or type a new file name in the Name text box.

- Choose an option from the Mode menu (RGB to keep the photos in color, or Grayscale to automatically make them black and white). If the file has an embedded ICC profile, you can choose the profile from the menu.

- For Resolution, accept the default (72) or type a new value. A higher resolution increases the file size.

- Select Anti-aliased to minimize the jagged edges as the image is rasterized (bitmapped).

5 Select Suppress Warnings to hide any error messages during the import process.

6 Click OK to open the file.

For information on placing a PDF file in a new layer, search on PDF in Help.

To close a file

1 Do one of the following:

- Choose File > Close.

- Choose File > Close All.

2 Choose whether or not to save the file:

- Click Yes to save the file.

- Click No to close the file without saving it.

Saving and exporting images

About saving images

After you edit an image, you need to save it or you'll lose your work. Usually you'll want to save an image that you are editing in the Photoshop (PSD) format to ensure that all the image data is preserved. Photoshop format doesn't compress your image data. Your digital camera may save photos in JPEG format, but it's better to use the Photoshop format rather than resave a photo in JPEG format unless you are ready to share it or use it on a web page. Each time you save in JPEG format, the image data is compressed, potentially causing some data to be lost. You may start to notice reduced image quality after 2-3 saves. The disadvantage of saving in Photoshop PSD format is that the file size will increase significantly because the file is not compressed.

Photoshop Elements can save images in several file formats. The file format you choose depends on how you plan to use it. If you are working with web images, the Save For Web command provides many options for optimizing images. If you need to convert several images to the same file format, or the same size and resolution, use the Process Multiple Files command.

To learn more about choosing file formats when you save a file, see "File formats for saving" in Help.

To save changes to the current file

1 Choose File > Save, or click the Save button 🖫 in the shortcuts bar.

2 To change save options such as the file name or format, choose File > Save As and set any of the following file saving options. Then click Save.

Note: Some file formats open another dialog box with additional options.

Save As Specifies the file name for the saved image.

Where Specifies the location for the saved image.

Format Specifies the file format for the saved image.

As a Copy Saves a copy of the file while keeping the current file open. The copy is saved to the folder containing the currently open file.

Layers Preserves all layers in the image. If this option is disabled or unavailable, there are no layers in the image. A warning icon ⚠ at the Layers check box indicates that the layers in your image will be flattened or merged for the selected format. To preserve layers, select another format.

Color Embed a color profile in the image for certain formats.

File formats for saving

Photoshop Elements can save images in the following file formats:

BMP A standard Windows image format. You can specify either Windows or OS/2 format and a bit depth for the image. For 4-bit and 8-bit images using Windows format, you can also specify RLE compression.

CompuServe GIF (Graphics Interchange Format) Commonly used to display graphics and small animations in web pages. GIF is a compressed format designed to minimize file size and transfer time. GIF supports only 8-bit color images (256 or fewer colors). You can also save an image as a GIF file using the Save For Web command. (See "To save a file in GIF format" in Help.)

JPEG (Joint Photographic Experts Group) Used to save photographs, JPEG format retains all color information in an image but compresses file size by selectively discarding data. You can choose the level of compression. Higher compression results in lower image quality and a smaller file size; lower compression results in better image quality and a larger file size. JPEG is a standard format for displaying images over the web. (See "To save a file in JPEG format" in Help.)

JPEG 2000 Produces images with better compression, quality, color management, and metadata capability than JPEG. JPEG 2000 also supports transparency in layered images and retains any saved selections. Photoshop Elements saves images in extended JPEG 2000 (JPX) format, which is a more comprehensive file format than standard JPEG 2000 (JP2). You can make files JP2 compatible by selecting an option in the JPEG 2000 dialog box. (See "To save a file in JPEG 2000 format" in Help.)

Photoshop (PSD) The standard Photoshop Elements format. You should generally use this format to save your work and preserve all your image data and layers.

PCX A bitmap format widely supported on a variety of platforms.

Photoshop PDF (Portable Document Format) A cross-platform and cross-application file format. PDF files accurately display and preserve fonts, page layouts, and both vector and bitmap graphics. (See "To save a file in Photoshop PDF format" in Help.)

Note: PDF and PDP are the same except that PDPs are opened in Adobe Photoshop® and PDFs are opened in Acrobat.

Photoshop EPS (Encapsulated PostScript) Used to share Photoshop files with many illustration and page-layout programs. For best results, print documents with EPS images to PostScript-enabled printers. (See "To save a file in Photoshop EPS format" in Help.)

PICT Used with Mac OS graphics and page-layout applications to transfer images between applications. PICT is especially effective at compressing images with large areas of solid color.

When saving an RGB image in PICT format, you can choose either 16-bit or 32-bit pixel resolution. For a grayscale image, you can choose from 2, 4, or 8 bits per pixel.

PiXAR Used for exchanging files with PiXAR image computers. PiXAR workstations are designed for high-end graphics applications, such as those used for three-dimensional images and animation. PiXAR format supports RGB and grayscale images.

PNG (Portable Network Graphics) Used for lossless compression and for display of images on the web. Unlike GIF, PNG supports 24-bit images and produces background transparency without jagged edges; however, some web browsers do not support PNG images. PNG preserves transparency in grayscale and RGB images. (See "To save a file in PNG format" in Help.)

Photoshop Raw Used for transferring images between applications and computer platforms when other formats won't work. Only existing camera raw format files can be saved in the Camera Raw format.

Scitex CT Used in the prepress industry.

TGA (Targa) Designed for systems using the Truevision video board. When saving an RGB image in this format, you can choose a pixel depth of 16, 24, or 32 bits per pixel and RLE compression.

TIFF (Tagged-Image File Format) Used to exchange files between applications and computer platforms. TIFF is a flexible bitmap image format supported by most paint, image-editing, and page-layout applications. Most desktop scanners can produce TIFF files. (See "To save a file in TIFF format" in Help.)

In addition, Photoshop Elements can open files in several other older formats: PS 2.0, Pixel Paint, Alias Pix, IFF format, Portable Bit Map, SGI RGB, Soft Image, Wavefront, RLA, ElectricImage.

To set file saving preferences

❖ Choose Photoshop Elements > Preferences > Saving Files, and set the following options.

Image Previews Saves a preview image with the file. Select Never Save to save files without previews, Always Save to save files with specified previews, or Ask When Saving to assign previews on a file-by-file basis.

Append File Extension Specifies an option for the three-character file extensions that indicate a file's format: Select Never if you don't want to include the format extension, Always if you always want the three-character extension added, or Ask When Saving if you want the flexibility to choose when the extension is added. The default setting is Always.

Ignore Camera Data (EXIF) Profiles Select this option to automatically discard any color profiles used by your digital camera. The color profile you use in Photoshop Elements is saved with the image.

Maximize PSD File Compatibility Saves a composite image in a layered Photoshop file so that it can be imported or opened by a wider range of applications: Select Never to skip this step, Always to automatically save the composite, or Ask if you'd like to be prompted each time you save a file.

Recent File List Contains: _ Files Specifies how many files are available in the File > Open Recently Edited File submenu. Enter a value from 0 to 30. The default value is 10.

Processing camera raw image files

About camera raw image files

A camera raw file contains unprocessed picture data from a camera's image sensor. Think of camera raw files as your photo negative. Many digital cameras can save raw format files. You can open a raw file in Photoshop Elements, process it, and save it—rather than relying on the camera to process the file. Working with camera raw files lets you set the proper white balance, tonal range, contrast, color saturation, and sharpening.

You can reprocess the file repeatedly to achieve the results you want. Photoshop Elements doesn't save your changes to the original raw file, but it saves the last setting you used to process it.

After processing the raw image file with the Camera Raw dialog box, you open the image in Photoshop Elements, where you can work with it in the same way that you work with any photo. Then, you can save the file in any format supported by Photoshop Elements. You should usually use PSD.

To use raw files, you need to set your camera to save files in its own raw file format. When you download the files from the camera, they have file extensions like NEF or CRW. Photoshop Elements can open raw files only from supported cameras. Visit the Adobe website to view a list of supported cameras.

For information on processing, editing, saving, and opening camera raw files, see Help.

Chapter 6: Using Layers

Creating layers

Understanding layers

Layers are useful because they let you add components to the image and work on them one at a time, without permanently changing your original image. For each layer, you can adjust color and brightness, apply special effects, reposition layer content, specify opacity and blending values, and so on. You can also rearrange the stacking order, link layers to work on them simultaneously, and create web animations with layers.

Layers are like stacked, transparent sheets of glass on which you can paint images. You can see through the transparent areas of a layer to the layers below. You can work on each layer independently, experimenting to create the effect you want. Each layer remains independent until you combine, or merge, the layers. The bottommost layer in the Layers palette, the Background layer, is always locked, or protected, meaning that you cannot change its stacking order, blending mode, or opacity (unless you convert it to a regular layer).

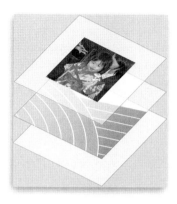

Transparent areas on a layer let you see through to the layers below.

Layers are organized in the Layers palette. It's a good idea to keep this palette visible whenever you're working in Photoshop Elements. With one glance, you can see the active layer (the selected layer that you are editing). You can link layers, so they move as a unit, helping you manage layers. Because multiple layers in an image increases the file size, you can reduce the file size by merging layers that you're done editing. The Layers palette is an important source of information as you edit photos. You can also use the Layer menu to work with layers.

Ordinary layers are pixel-based, or image, layers. There are several other layer types you can use to create special effects:

Fill layers Contain a color gradient, solid color, or pattern.

Adjustment layers Enable you to fine-tune color, brightness, and saturation without making permanent changes to your image (until you flatten, or collapse the adjustment layer). For more information about adjustment layers, see Help.

Type layers and shape layers Let you create vector-based text and shapes. For more information about type layers and shape layers, see Help.

You can't paint on an adjustment layer, although you can paint on its mask. To paint on fill or type layers, you first convert them to regular image layers.

For information about adjustment and fill layers, opacity, and blending modes, see Help.

About the Layers palette

The Layers palette in the Editor (Window > Layers) lists all layers in an image, in stacking order from the top layer to the Background layer at the bottom. You can drag the palette by its title out of the Palette Bin to keep it visible as you work with it.

The active layer, or the layer that you are working on, is highlighted blue for easy identification. As you work in an image, it's a good idea to check which layer is active to make sure that the adjustments and edits you perform affect the correct layer. For example, if you choose a command and nothing seems to happen, check to make sure that you're looking at the active layer.

Using the icons in the palette, you can accomplish many tasks—such as creating, hiding, linking, locking, and deleting a layer. With some exceptions, your changes affect only the selected, or active, layer, which is highlighted.

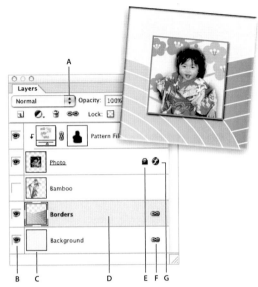

Layers palette
A. Blending mode menu **B.** *Show/Hide layer* **C.** *Layer thumbnail*
D. Highlighted layer is active layer **E.** *Locked layer* **F.** *Layer is linked to another layer* **G.** *Layer has style applied*

In the list of layers, the palette shows a thumbnail, a title, and one or more icons that give information about each layer:

👁 The layer is visible. Click the eye to show or hide a layer. (Hidden layers are not printed.)

🔗 The layer is linked to the active layer.

🔒 The layer is locked.

📁 The image contains layer groups and was imported from Photoshop. Photoshop Elements doesn't support layer groups and displays them in their collapsed state. You must simplify them to create an editable image.

You use the buttons at the top of the palette to perform actions:

▣ Create a new layer.

⬤ Create a new fill or adjustment layer.

🗑 Delete a layer.

🔗 The layer is linked to another layer.

▢ Lock transparency.

🔒 Lock all layers.

Also at the top are the palette Blending Mode menu (Normal, Dissolve, Darken, and so on), an Opacity text box, and a More button displaying a menu of layer commands and palette options.

Adding layers

Newly added layers appear above the selected layer in the Layers palette. You can add layers to an image by using any of the following methods:

• Creating new, blank layers or turning selections into layers.

• Converting a background into a regular layer or vice versa.

• Pasting selections into the image.

• Using the Type tool or a shape tool.

• Duplicating an existing layer.

You can create up to 8000 layers in an image, each with its own blending mode and opacity. However, memory constraints may lower this limit.

To create and name a new blank layer

❖ Do any of the following in the Editor:

• To create a new layer with default name and settings, click the New Layer button ▣ at the top of the Layers palette. The resulting layer uses Normal mode with 100% opacity, and is named according to its creation order. (To rename the new layer, double-click it and type a new name.

• To create a new layer and specify a name and options, choose Layer > New > Layer or choose New Layer from the More menu in the Layers palette. Specify a name and other options, and then click OK.

The new layer is automatically selected and appears in the palette above the layer that was last selected.

To convert the Background layer to a regular layer

The Background layer is the bottom-most layer in an image. Other layers stack on top of the Background, which usually (but not always) contains the actual image data of a photo. To protect the image, the Background layer is always locked. If you want to change its stacking order, blending mode, or opacity, you must first convert it to a regular layer.

1 In the Editor, do one of the following:

• Double-click the Background layer in the Layers palette.

• Choose Layer > New > Layer From Background.

• Select the Background layer, and choose Duplicate Layer from the More menu in the Layers palette to leave the Background layer intact and create a copy of it as a new layer.

You can create a duplicate layer of the converted background layer, no matter how you convert the layer; simply select the converted background layer and choose Duplicate Layer from the More menu.

2 To rename the converted layer, Control-click it, choose Rename Layer, type a new name, and click OK.

If you drag the Background Eraser tool on the Background layer, it is automatically converted to a regular layer, and erased areas become transparent.

Editing layers

To select a layer

Any changes you make to an image affect only the active layer. If you don't see the desired results when you manipulate an image, make sure that the correct layer is selected.

❖ In the Editor, do one of the following:

- In the Layers palette, select a layer's thumbnail or name.

- To select more than one layer, hold down Command and click each layer.

- Select the Move tool ⊹ , Control-click in the image, and choose a layer from the context menu. The context menu lists all the layers that contain pixels under the current pointer location, and all adjustment layers.

To select layers interactively as you use the Move tool, select Auto Select Layer in the options bar. When you select this option, the Move tool selects the topmost layer containing opaque pixels under the pointer.

For information on copying and arranging layers, see Help.

To show or hide a layer

In the Layers palette, the eye icon 👁 in the leftmost column next to a layer means that the layer is visible.

1 In the Editor, choose Window > Layers if the Layers palette is not already open.

2 Do one of the following:

- To hide a layer, click its eye icon. Click in the eye column again to show the layer.

- Drag through the eye column to show or hide more than one layer.

- To display just one layer, Option-click the eye icon for that layer. Option-click in the eye column again to show all the layers.

To lock or unlock a layer

You can fully or partially lock layers to protect their contents. When a layer is locked, a lock icon appears to the right of the layer name, and the layer cannot be deleted. Except for the background layer, you can move locked layers to different locations in the stacking order of the Layers palette.

❖ In the Editor, select the layer in the Layers palette, and do one of the following:

- Click the Lock All icon 🔒 at the top of the Layers palette to lock all layer properties. Click the icon again to unlock them.

- Click the Lock Transparency icon ☐ at the top of the Layers palette to lock the transparent areas of the layer, so that no painting occurs in them. Click the icon again to unlock.

Note: For type and shape layers, transparency is locked by default and cannot be unlocked without first simplifying the layer.

To rename a layer

As you add layers to an image, it's helpful to rename layers according to their content. Use descriptive layer names so that you can easily identify layers in the Layers palette.

Note: You can't rename the Background layer unless you change it to a normal layer.

❖ In the Editor, double-click the layer's name in the Layers palette, and enter a new name.

To simplify a layer

You simplify a type layer, shape layer, solid color layer, gradient layer, or pattern fill layer (or a layer group imported from Photoshop) by converting it to an image layer. You need to simplify these layers before you can apply filters to them or edit them with the painting tools. However, you can no longer use the type- and shape-editing options on simplified layers.

1 In the Editor, select a type layer, shape layer, fill layer, or a Photoshop layer group from the Layers palette.

2 Simplify the layer or imported layer group:

• If you selected a shape layer, click Simplify in the options bar.

• If you selected a type, shape, or fill layer, or a Photoshop layer group, choose Simplify Layer from

either the Layer menu or the Layers palette More menu.

To delete a layer

Deleting layers that you no longer need reduces the size of your image file.

1 In the Editor, select the layer in the Layers palette.

2 Do one of the following:

• Drag the layer to the Delete Layer button 🗑 at the top of the Layers palette.

• Click the Delete Layer button at the top of the Layers palette, and click Yes in the delete confirmation dialog box. To bypass this dialog box, press Option as you click the Delete button.

• Choose Delete Layer from either the Layer menu or the Layers palette More menu, and click Yes.

Chapter 7: Selecting parts of an image

Making selections

About selections

A selection defines the editable area in a photo (for example, you might want to lighten one part of a photo without affecting the rest). You can make a selection with either a selection tool or a selection command. A selection border, which you can hide, surrounds the selection. You can change, copy, or delete pixels inside the selection border, but you can't touch areas outside the selection border until you deselect the selection.

Photoshop Elements contains several selection tools that suit different kinds of selections. For example, the Elliptical Marquee tool selects circular and elliptical areas, and the Magic Wand tool can select an area of similar colors with one click. More complex selections can be made with one of the Lasso tools. You can even smooth the edges of a selection with feathering and anti-aliasing.

Note: *Selections are limited to the active layer—to make changes to all layers at once, you first need to flatten the image. (See "To flatten an image" in Help.)*

Selection made with Elliptical Marquee tool, color adjusted in selected area

For more information about selections, including smoothing selections and saving selections, see Help.

About the selection tools

The selection tools are located in the toolbox, by default positioned on the left side of your screen.

Rectangular Marquee tool *Draws square or rectangular selection borders.*

Elliptical Marquee tool *Draws round or elliptical selection borders.*

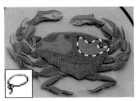

Lasso tool *Draws freehand selection borders. This tool is great for making very precise selections.*

Polygonal Lasso tool *Draws multiple straight-edged segments of a selection border.*

Magnetic Lasso tool *Draws a selection border that automatically snaps to edges you drag over in the photo.*

Magic Wand tool *Selects pixels of similar color with one click.*

Magic Selection Brush tool *Automatically makes a selection based on color and texture when you draw or click an area.*

Selection Brush tool *Automatically selects or deselects the area you paint, depending on whether you're in Selection or Mask mode.*

For information on selecting and deselecting using commands, see Help.

To use the Rectangular and Elliptical Marquee tools

The Rectangular Marquee tool draws square or rectangular selection borders, and the Elliptical Marquee tool draws round or elliptical selection borders.

Rectangular and Elliptical Marquee tool options
A. Rectangular Marquee tool **B.** *Elliptical Marquee tool* **C.** *New selection* **D.** *Add to selection* **E.** *Subtract from a selection* **F.** *Intersect with a selection*

1 In the Editor, select the Rectangular Marquee tool ⬚ or the Elliptical Marquee tool ◯ in the toolbox.

2 (Optional) Set marquee tool options in the options bar located above your image:

• Specify whether to create a new selection, add to a selection, subtract from a selection, or select an area intersected by other selections.

• To soften the selection border so that it blends into the area outside the selection, enter a Feather value.

• To smooth the edges of your selection, select Anti-aliased (Elliptical Marquee tool only).

• From the Mode pop-up menu, choose Normal to visually set the size and proportions of the selection border; Fixed Aspect Ratio to set a width-to-height ratio for the selection border; or Fixed Size to specify the marquee's height and width.

3 Drag over the area you want to select. Hold down the Shift key as you drag to constrain the selection marquee to a square or circle.

💡 *To reposition a marquee tool selection border, hold down the spacebar as you drag with the selection tool. Release the spacebar once the selection border is in the correct area.*

To use the Lasso tool

The Lasso tool draws freehand selection borders. This tool lets you make very precise selections.

Lasso tool options
A. Lasso tool **B.** *Magnetic Lasso tool* **C.** *Polygonal Lasso tool* **D.** *New selection* **E.** *Add to selection* **F.** *Subtract from selection* **G.** *Intersect with selection*

1 In the Editor, select the Lasso tool ◯ from the toolbox. (If you don't see it in the toolbox, select either the Magnetic Lasso tool or the Polygonal Lasso tool, and then click the Lasso tool icon in the options bar.)

2 (Optional) Set Lasso tool options in the options bar located above your image:

• Specify whether to create a new selection, add to an existing selection, subtract from a selection, or select an area intersected by other selections.

• To soften the selection border so that it blends into the area outside the selection, enter a Feather value.

• To smooth the edges of your selection, select Anti-aliased.

3 Drag to draw a freehand selection border:

• To add to the selection, release the mouse; then press Shift and when the pointer changes to 🔄, drag.

• To subtract from the selection, release the mouse; then press Option and when the pointer changes to 🔄, drag.

• To add straight-edge segments, press Option (while pressing the mouse); then release the mouse, and when the pointer changes to ◯ , click where you want to position the end of the segment.

4 To close the selection border, release the mouse button. A straight selection segment is drawn from where you released the mouse button to the starting point of your selection.

To use the Polygonal Lasso tool

The Polygonal Lasso tool draws straight-edged segments of a selection border. You can create as many segments as you need to draw a selection border.

Polygonal Lasso tool options
A. Lasso tool B. Magnetic Lasso tool C. Polygonal Lasso tool
D. New selection E. Add to selection F. Subtract from selection
G. Intersect with selection

1 In the Editor, select the Polygonal Lasso tool ⬚ from the toolbox. (If you don't see it in the toolbox, select either the Magnetic Lasso tool or the Lasso tool, and then click the Polygonal tool icon in the options bar.)

2 (Optional) Set Polygonal Lasso tool options in the options bar located above your image:

- Specify whether to create a new selection, add to an existing selection, subtract from a selection, or select an area intersected by other selections.

- To soften the selection border so that it blends into the area outside the selection, enter a Feather value.

- To smooth the edges of your selection, select Anti-aliased.

3 Click where you want the first straight segment to begin, and click a second time where you want the segment to end and the next one to begin. Continue clicking to create segments.

If you make a mistake, press the Delete key to erase segments.You can switch from creating straight-edge segments to drawing freehand by pressing Option.

4 Close the selection border by doing one of the following:

- Position the pointer over the starting point and click. A closed circle appears next to the pointer when you are over the starting point.

- If the pointer is not over the starting point, double-click, or Command-click. A straight selection segment is drawn from your pointer to the starting point of your selection.

To use the Magnetic Lasso tool

The Magnetic Lasso tool draws a selection border that automatically snaps to edges of objects you drag over in the photo. This makes it easy to draw precise selection borders. The Magnetic Lasso tool ⬚ is useful for quickly selecting objects with complex edges set against high-contrast backgrounds.

Magnetic Lasso tool options
A. Lasso tool B. Magnetic Lasso tool C. Polygonal Lasso tool
D. New selection E. Add to selection F. Subtract from selection
G. Intersect with selection

1 In the Editor, select the Magnetic Lasso tool from the toolbox. (If you don't see it in the toolbox, select either the Lasso tool or the Polygonal Lasso tool, and then click the Magnetic tool icon in the options bar.)

2 (Optional) Set Magnetic Lasso tool options in the options bar located above your image:

• Specify whether to create a new selection, add to an existing selection, subtract from a selection, or select an area intersected by other selections.

• To soften the selection border so that it blends into the area outside the selection, enter a Feather value.

• To smooth the edges of your selection, select Anti-aliased.

• To specify the area of edge detection, enter a pixel value between 1 and 256 for Width. The tool detects edges only within the specified distance from the pointer.

To change the Magnetic Lasso pointer so that it indicates the area of edge detection (the Width value), press the Caps Lock key.

• To specify the Magnetic Lasso tool's sensitivity to edges in the photo, enter a value between 1% and 100% for Edge Contrast. A higher value detects only edges that contrast sharply with their surroundings; a lower value detects lower-contrast edges.

• To specify the rate at which the Magnetic Lasso tool sets fastening points, enter a value between 0 and 100 for Frequency. A higher value anchors the selection border in place more quickly.

3 Add segments of a selection border by doing one of the following:

• Click points along the edge.

• Drag along the edge while pressing the mouse button.

The selection border snaps to the edge in the photo. If the border doesn't snap to the desired edge, click once to add a point manually; then continue tracing the border and clicking points as needed. If you make a mistake, press the Delete key to erase points along the border.

4 Close the selection border by doing one of the following:

• To close the border manually, drag back over the starting point and click. A closed circle appears next to the pointer when you are over the starting point.

• To close the border with a freehand magnetic segment, double-click or press Enter.

• To close the border with a straight segment, double-click while pressing Option.

To switch between the Magnetic Lasso and other lasso tools

❖ With the Magnetic Lasso tool selected, do one of the following:

• To activate the Lasso tool, Option-drag.

• To activate the Polygonal Lasso tool, Option-click.

To use the Magic Wand tool

The Magic Wand tool selects pixels within a similar color range with one click. You specify the color range, or tolerance, for the Magic Wand tool's selection. Use the Magic Wand tool when you have an area of similar colors, like a blue sky.

Magic Wand tool options
A. New selection B. Add to selection C. Subtract from selection
D. Intersect with selection

1 In the Editor, select the Magic Wand tool .

2 (Optional) Set Magic Wand tool options in the options bar located above your image:

- For Tolerance, enter a value between 0 to 255. Enter a low value to select colors very similar to the pixel you click, or enter a higher value to select a broader range of colors.

- To define a smooth selection edge, select Anti-aliased.

- To select only adjacent areas using the same colors, select Contiguous. When this option is deselected, pixels using the same colors are selected throughout the entire photo.

- To select colors using data from all the visible layers, select Use All Layers. When this option is deselected, the Magic Wand tool selects colors from only the active layer.

3 In the photo, click the color you want to select.

4 To add to the selection, Shift+click unselected areas. To remove an area from the selection, Option+click the area you want to remove.

To use the Magic Selection Brush tool

The Magic Selection Brush tool makes a selection based on color and texture similarity when you draw, scribble, or click the area you want to select. The mark you make doesn't need to be precise, because when you release the mouse, Photoshop Elements draws the selection border.

Magic Selection Brush tool options
*A. Magic Selection Brush tool **B.** Selection Brush tool **C.** New selection **D.** Indicate Foreground **E.** Indicate Background*

1 In the Editor, select the Magic Selection Brush tool ✎.

2 In the options bar, choose an option:

New Selection Lets you draw a new selection. This option is selected by default.

Indicate Foreground Lets you add to an existing selection

Indicate Background Lets you subtract from an existing selection. This option is only available after you make a selection.

3 Choose a brush size from the Size menu in the options bar. If you want to scribble over a large area, you can use a larger brush. For a smaller area, choose a smaller brush size to keep the selection marks inside the area.

4 Click an area or draw a line that covers the range of colors in the object you want to select, and then release the mouse button.

The selection border appears.

5 Do any of the following to refine the selection:

- To add to the selection, click the Indicate Foreground brush ✎ in the options bar and click or drag across the area you want to add. By default this brush draws red lines and becomes the active brush after you make a new selection.

- To remove an area from the selection, click the Indicate Background brush ✎ in the options bar and click or drag across the area you want to subtract from the selection. By default this brush draws blue lines.

Note: You can change the color for these brushes by selecting the brush and choosing a new color from the Color menu in the options bar.

- Use the Selection Brush tool to fine-tune the selection.

- To start a new selection, click the New Selection brush ✏ in the options bar and click or draw to specify the new selection area.

To use the Selection Brush tool

The Selection Brush tool makes selections two ways: you can paint over the area you want to select in Selection mode, or you can paint over areas you don't want to select using a semi-opaque overlay in Mask mode.

You can first make a rough selection with a marquee tool, Magic Selection Brush, or other selection tool, and then fine-tune your selection with the Selection Brush tool. You can add to the selection using the Selection Brush tool in the Selection mode, or subtract from it in Mask mode.

Selection Brush tool options
A. *Magic Selection Brush tool* **B.** *Selection Brush tool* **C.** *Add to selection* **D.** *Subtract from selection* **E.** *Brush preset pop-up palette* **F.** *Brush size*

1 In the Editor, select the Selection Brush tool 🖌 from the toolbox. You may need to click the Magic Selection Brush tool in the toolbox and select the

Selection Brush from the list of hidden tools that appears.

2 By default, the tool is set to Add To Selection 🔲 . To subtract from the selection at any time, click Subtract From Selection 🔲 in the options bar.

3 (Optional) Set Selection Brush tool options in the options bar located above your image:

- Choose a brush from the brush presets pop-up palette.

- Specify the brush size.

- Choose Selection (to add to the selection) or Mask (to subtract from the selection) from the Mode menu.

- Set the brush tip's hardness to a value between 1 percent and 100 percent.

💡 *If you use a soft-edged brush with the Selection Brush tool, changing the Mode option to Mask can help you see the soft edges of the selection.*

- When using Mask mode, specify an Overlay Opacity between 1 percent and 100 percent.

- When using Mask mode, click the Overlay Color swatch and select a color in the Color Picker to set the mask color. This is useful when the mask color (Overlay Color) is too similar to the colors in the photo.

4 Draw in your photo to select or deselect areas.

Adding to a selection while in Selection mode (left), and subtracting from a selection while in Mask mode (right)

To use the Magic Extractor

Use the Magic Extractor to make accurate selections by extracting the foreground and background areas that you specify. You can specify these areas by placing colored dots in the areas you want to mark. After you mark the areas and close the dialog box, only the foreground area appears in the photo in the Editor.

The Magic Extractor makes it easy to extract people or objects so that you can select the person or object and superimpose them onto other backgrounds. For example, you can extract yourself from a photo of you on your bicycle at home, and superimpose it on a photo of cyclists in the Tour de France. You can save the extracted image as a file that you can use again and again.

Using the Magic Extractor
A. Area you want to extract marked with red dots **B.** *Background marked with blue dots* **C.** *Extracted image*

To see a color version of this image, see Figure 7-1 in the color section.

1 In the Editor, open the photo containing the object you want to extract.

2 To limit what appears in the Magic Extractor dialog box, make a preliminary selection using any selection tool.

3 Choose Image > Magic Extractor.

The Magic Extractor dialog box opens with the Foreground Brush tool 🖌 selected by default.

4 Click multiple times or draw lines to mark the area you want to extract.

5 Click the Background Brush tool 🖌 and click multiple times or draw lines to mark the area that you do not want included in your selection. The more points you add, the longer it will take to calculate a preview.

💡 *When selecting objects with varied colors and textures, drag across all the colors and textures to ensure a more accurate selection.*

6 To help mark your selection, use the Zoom tool 🔍 or the Hand tool 🖐 to magnify and navigate around the photo. Press Option as you use the Zoom tool to zoom out.

7 To specify a different brush size or color, do any of the following:

• Choose a new size from the Brush Size menu.

• Click the Foreground Color or Background Color swatch and choose a new color in the color picker, and then click OK.

8 Click Preview to see the current selection.

9 To specify preview settings, do any of the following:

• To change what is displayed in the preview area, choose either Selection Area or Original Photo from the Display menu. Or press x on your keyboard to toggle back and forth between the two views.

• To specify a different background, choose an option from the Background menu.

10 Do any of the following to fine-tune the selection, and then preview the results again:

• To add to or subtract from the selection, draw more dots or lines using either the Foreground or Background tool.

• To erase foreground or background dots, select the Point Eraser tool 🖉 and click or drag over the marks you want to remove.

• To add areas to a selection, select the Add To Selection tool 🖉 and click or drag over the area you want to add.

• To remove areas from the selection, select the Remove From Selection tool 🖉 and drag over the areas you want to remove.

• To smooth the edges of your foreground selection, select the Smoothing Brush tool 🖌 and drag over the areas you want to smooth.

• To soften the edges of your selection, specify a higher value in the Feather box.

• To fill remaining holes in the main selection, click Fill Holes.

• To separate and remove an area from the main selection, select the Remove From Selection Tool 🖉 and drag a line between the main selection and the area you want to remove. Then click Fill Holes.

• To remove fringe colors left between the foreground and background, click Defringe. To increase or decrease the amount of fringe removed, specify a value from the Defringe Width menu.

11 If you want to start over, click Reset to remove all marks.

12 Click OK to accept the extraction.

To delete a selected area

If you delete a selection on a background layer or a layer that uses the Lock Transparency option, the selected area is replaced with the background color or checkerboard background pattern.

❖ In the Editor, do any of the following:

- Choose Edit > Delete to remove the selection. (If you delete a selection by mistake, you can choose Edit > Undo to get it back.)

- Press the Delete key to remove the selection.

- Choose Edit > Cut to cut the selection to the Clipboard. You can then paste it elsewhere.

For more information, see "Understanding layers" on page 47 and "To lock or unlock a layer" on page 50.

Modifying selections

To move a selection border

Moving a selection border repositions just the border without altering the photo.

1 Using any selection tool in the Editor, click New Selection ▢ in the options bar, and position the pointer inside an existing selection border. The pointer changes to indicate that you can move the selection ▸₊.

Note: The New Selection option appears in the options bar when any selection tool is selected—except the Selection Brush tool. Switch to another selection tool temporarily, if necessary, to select this option.

2 Do one of the following:

- Drag the border to enclose a different area of the photo. You can drag a selection border beyond the canvas boundaries; however, this makes it hard to get back. You can also drag the selection border to another image window or to an image in the Photo Bin.

- To move the selection in 1-pixel increments, use an arrow key.

- To move the selection in 10-pixel increments, hold down Shift, and use an arrow key.

- To constrain the direction to multiples of 45°, begin dragging, and then hold down Shift as you continue to drag.

For more information, see "To move a selection" on page 64.

To invert a selection

Inverting a selection changes the unselected areas into selected areas, protecting the area you previously selected.

❖ In a photo with an existing selection border, choose Select > Inverse.

💡 *You can use this command to easily select an object that appears against a solid-colored area. Select the solid color using the Magic Wand tool, and then choose Select > Inverse.*

To add to or subtract from a selection

You can add to or subtract from an existing selection to fine-tune selection borders. For instance, you could make a donut-shaped selection by first making a circular selection and then subtracting a circular selection within it.

❖ In the Editor, select a selection tool, and do one of the following:

- Hold down Shift (a plus sign appears next to the pointer) to add to the selection, or hold down Option to subtract (a minus sign appears next to the pointer). Then select the area to add or subtract and make another selection.

- Click Add To Selection 🔲 or Subtract From Selection 🔲 in the options bar, and make another selection. (The Add To Selection and Subtract From Selection options appear in the options bar when any selection tool is selected.)

For information on modifying a selection, including feathering and anti-aliasing, see Help.

To defringe a selection

When you move or paste a selection, some of the pixels surrounding the selection border are included with the selection. These extra pixels can result in a fringe or halo around the edges of the selection. The Defringe Layer command replaces the color of any fringe pixels with the colors of nearby pixels containing pure colors (those without background color). For example, if you select a yellow object on a blue background and then move the selection, some of the blue background is moved with the object. Defringe replaces the blue pixels with yellow pixels.

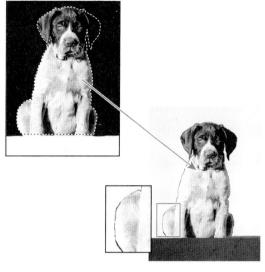

Dog selected and copied to a new image where artifacts from the dark background are visible (top). Image after using the Defringe Layer command (bottom).

To see a color version of this image, see Figure 7-2 in the color section.

1 Copy and paste a selection into a new or existing layer.

2 Choose Enhance > Adjust Color > Defringe Layer.

3 In the Defringe dialog box, type the number of pixels you'd like to replace around the object. A value of 1 or 2 should be sufficient.

4 Click OK.

For information on smoothing selection edges, see Help.

Moving and copying selections

To move a selection

The Move tool ▸⊕ lets you cut and drag a pixel selection to a new location in the photo. You can also use the tool to move or copy selections between photos in Photoshop Elements and photos in other applications.

Moving a selection from one photo into another using the Move tool

To activate the Move tool when another tool is selected, hold down Command. (This technique does not work with the Hand tool.)

1 In the Editor, select the Move tool ▸⊕ from the toolbox.

2 (Optional) Set Move tool options in the options bar:

Auto Select Layer Selects the topmost layer that has pixels under the Move tool, rather than the selected layer.

Show Bounding Box Displays the bounding box around the selected item.

3 Move the pointer inside the selection border, and drag the selection to a new position. If you've selected multiple areas, all pixel selections move as you drag.

Copying selections or layers

You can copy and paste selections using the Move tool or the Copy, Copy Merged, Cut, Paste, or Paste Into Selection commands in the Edit menu.

Keep in mind that when a selection or layer is pasted between photos with different resolutions, the pasted data retains its original pixel dimensions. This can make the pasted portion appear out of proportion to the new image. Use the Image Size command to make the source and destination photos the same resolution before copying and pasting.

Selections that you cut or copy are stored on the Clipboard. Only one selection is stored on the Clipboard at a time.

When you exit Photoshop Elements, anything in the Clipboard is lost unless Export Clipboard is selected in the General Preferences.

For more information about copying and saving selections, see Help.

To paste one selection into another

You can use the Paste Into Selection command to paste one selection into another. This command lets you take advantage of elements within the selected area, and prevent the pasted image from looking flat and unnatural. For instance, you can use a Hard Light blending mode at 85% opacity to retain the reflection in a pair of sunglasses. When using blending modes this way, you need to create a new layer and paste the selection into that layer.

A   B

C

Copying a selection from one image to another
A. *Part of original photo selected* **B.** *Photo to copy and paste into original* **C.** *Resulting image*

1 In the Editor, use the Copy command to copy the part of the photo you want to paste. (You can even copy from photos in other applications.)

2 Make a selection in the photo into which you want to paste the copied photo.

3 Choose Edit > Paste Into Selection.

Note: The copied photo appears only within the selection border. You can move the copied photo within the border, but if you move it completely out of the border, it won't be visible.

4 With your pointer within the selection border, drag the pasted image to the proper location.

5 When you're satisfied with the results, deselect the pasted image to commit the changes.

To activate the Move tool when another tool is selected, hold down Command. (This technique does not work with the Hand tool.)

Chapter 8: Correcting and understanding color

Color correction basics

Color correction overview

Photoshop Elements provides several tools and commands for fixing the tonal range, color, and sharpness in your photos, and for removing dust spots or other defects. You can work in one of three workspaces, depending on your experience and needs.

Quick Fix If you are new to digital imaging, Quick Fix is a good place to start fixing photos. It has many of the basic tools for correcting color and lighting. (See "To correct color in Quick Fix" on page 67.)

Standard Edit (the Editor) If you've worked with images before, you'll find that the Standard Edit workspace provides the most flexible and powerful image-correction environment. It has the lighting and color-correction commands, along with tools for fixing image defects, making selections, adding text, and painting on your images.

When working with some of the adjustment commands in the Editor, you can make adjustments directly on the image pixels. Or you can use adjustment layers to make nondestructive adjustments that you can easily tweak until your image is right. (These commands are also available in the Quick Fix workspace, although you cannot use them with adjustment layers.)

Camera Raw If you shoot digital images in your camera's raw format, you can open and correct raw files in the Camera Raw dialog box. Camera raw files haven't been processed by your camera. You adjust the color and exposure to get the best image. Often you won't have to make other adjustments in Photoshop Elements. To open camera raw files in Photoshop Elements, first save them in a supported file format. (See "About camera raw image files" on page 45.)

 For information on color basics and color management, see these topics in Help.

To correct color in Quick Fix

Quick Fix conveniently assembles many of the basic photo fixing tools in Photoshop Elements. As you work in Quick Fix, you should limit the number of color and lighting controls that you apply to a photo. Generally, you use only one of the Auto controls on a photo. If that control doesn't achieve what you want, click the Reset button and try another one. You can also adjust your image using the slider controls, whether you've used an Auto control or not. Sharpening is the last fix you should perform on an image.

1 With a photo open in Standard Edit, click the Quick Fix button.

Any photos that you have stored in the Photo Bin are accessible while you are in Quick Fix.

2 (Optional) Set preview options by making a selection from the View menu (located under the image preview). You can set the preview to show how the photo looks before or after you make a fix, or to show both previews side-by-side.

3 (Optional) Use the Quick Fix tools to zoom, move, or crop the image, or to fix red eye. These tools work the same way in Quick Fix and the Editor.

Zoom tool 🔍 Sets the magnification of the preview image. Controls and options work like the Zoom tool in the toolbox. (See "To zoom in or out" on page 26.)

Hand tool ✋ Moves the image around in the preview window if the entire image is not visible. Press the spacebar to access the Hand tool when another tool is selected. (See "Viewing images in Standard Edit or Quick Fix" on page 25.)

Magic Selection Brush tool ✏ Selects portions of the image based on where you click or drag the tool. (See "To use the Magic Selection Brush tool" on page 58.)

Selection Brush tool ✏ Selects portions of an image that you paint with the brush, or selects the areas that are left unpainted. (See "To use the Selection Brush tool" on page 59.)

Crop tool ⊞ Removes part of an image. Drag with the tool in the preview image to select the portion you want to keep, and then press Enter. (See "To crop an image" on page 77.)

Red Eye Removal tool ⊙ Removes red eye in flash photos of people and green or white eye in pets. Drag the tool in the preview image around an eye you want

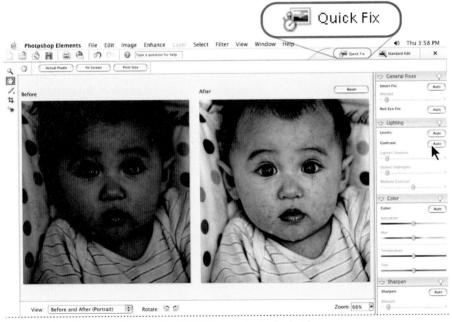

Using the Auto Contrast adjustment in Quick Fix to instantly fix the photo

to fix, or click the Auto button in the options bar. (See "To remove red eye" on page 87.)

4 To rotate the image in 90 degree increments, click either the Rotate Left or Rotate Right button at the bottom of the window.

5 Set any of the image fixing options on the right side of the window. Click the Reset button if you don't get the result you are looking for, and then try the other controls.

Smart Fix Adjusts lighting and color. Smart Fix corrects overall color balance and improves shadow and highlight detail, if necessary. The Smart Fix slider allows you to vary the amount of the adjustment. Click the Auto button to apply this command.

Red Eye Fix Automatically finds and fixes red eyes in the image.

Levels Adjusts the overall contrast of an image and may affect its color. If your image needs more contrast and it has a color cast, try this command, which works by individually mapping the lightest and darkest pixels in each color channel to black and white. Click the Auto button to apply this command. (See "About Levels adjustments" on page 72.)

Contrast Adjusts the overall contrast of an image without affecting its color. Use Auto Contrast when your image needs more contrast but the colors look right. Auto Contrast maps the lightest and darkest pixels in the image to white and black, which makes highlights appear lighter and shadows appear darker. Click the Auto button to apply this command.

Lighten Shadows Drag the slider to lighten the darkest areas of your photo without affecting the highlights. Pure black areas are not affected.

Darken Highlights Drag the slider to darken the lightest areas of your photo without affecting the shadows. Pure white areas are not affected.

Midtone Contrast Adjusts the contrast within the middle tonal values (those that are about half way between pure white and pure black) without affecting the extreme highlights and shadows.

Color Adjusts the contrast and color by identifying shadows, midtones, and highlights in the image rather than in individual color channels. It neutralizes the midtones and clips the white and black pixels using a default set of values. Click the Auto button to apply this command.

See Figure 8-1 in the color section.

Saturation Makes colors more vivid or more muted.

Hue Shifts all colors in an image. This control is best used in small amounts or with selected objects whose color you want to change.

Temperature Makes colors warmer (red) or cooler (blue). Use this control to enhance sunsets or skin tones, or when the color balance set by your camera is off.

Tint Makes color more green or magenta. Use this control to fine-tune the colors after using the Temperature control.

Sharpen Sharpens your photo. Click Auto Sharpen to use the default amount of sharpening. Drag the slider to vary the amount of sharpening. Zoom your preview to 100% to get a more accurate view of the amount of sharpening you are applying.

Correcting color in Standard Edit

If you've worked with images before, you'll find that the Editor workspace provides the most flexible and powerful image-correction environment. It has the lighting and color-correction commands, along with tools for fixing image defects, making selections, adding text, and painting on your images. When working with some of the adjustment commands in the Editor, you can make adjustments directly on the image pixels. Or you can use adjustment layers to make nondestructive adjustments that you can easily tweak until your image is right.

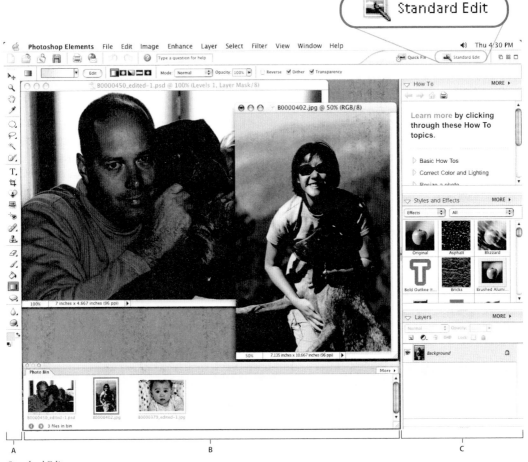

Standard Edit
A. *There are many tools for correcting problems and selecting portions of a photo.* **B.** *The Photo Bin lets you see which photos are open in the Editor.* **C.** *The Palette Bin holds palettes that you use to transform and enhance photos.*

As you work on your photos in the Editor, perform the following tasks in the order listed:

1. Specify a color management option

Specify color management options. (See "To set up color management" in Help.)

2. View the image at 100% and crop if necessary

Before making any color corrections, view the image at a zoom percentage of 100%. At 100%, Photoshop Elements displays the image most accurately. You can also check for image defects, such as dust spots or scratches. If you plan to crop the file, do it now to save on memory requirements and to ensure that the histogram uses only relevant information.

3. Check the scan quality and tonal range

Look at the image's histogram to evaluate whether the image has sufficient detail to produce high-quality output. (See "To view a histogram" in Help.)

4. Resize your image, if necessary

Resize your image to the size that you need if you are going to use it in another application or project. If you are going to print the image, you generally don't need to resize it. (See "About image size and resolution" on page 81.)

5. Adjust the highlights and shadows

Begin corrections by adjusting the values of the extreme highlight and shadow pixels in the image (also known as the tonal range). Setting an overall tonal range allows for the most detail possible throughout the image. This process is known as

setting the highlight and shadow or setting the white and black points. (See "About Levels adjustments" on page 72.)

6. Adjust the color balance

After correcting the tonal range, you can adjust the image's color balance to remove unwanted color casts or to correct oversaturated or undersaturated colors. With some Photoshop Elements Auto commands, both the tonal range and color are corrected in one step. (See "Adjusting saturation and hue" on page 75.)

7. Make other special color adjustments

Once you have corrected the overall color balance of your image, you can make optional adjustments to enhance colors. For example, you can increase the vividness of color in your image by increasing its saturation.

8. Retouch the image

Use the retouching tools, like the Spot Healing Brush, to remove any dust spots or defects in the image. (See "To remove spots and imperfections" on page 87.)

9. Sharpen the edges of the image

As a final step, use the Unsharp Mask filter to sharpen the clarity of edges in the image. This step helps restore detail and sharpness that tonal adjustments may reduce. (See "To use Unsharp Mask to sharpen an image" in Help.)

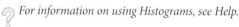 *For information on using Histograms, see Help.*

Using auto correct commands

Photoshop Elements provides several automatic lighting and color-correction commands in both Standard Edit and Quick Fix. The command you choose depends on your image. You can experiment with each of the auto commands. If you don't like the result of one, undo the command by choosing Edit > Undo, and try another command. You will rarely need to use more than one auto command to fix an image.

In the Editor, you access these commands in the Enhance menu. Use the auto command that best meets the needs of your image:

Auto Smart Fix Corrects overall color balance and improves shadow and highlight detail, if necessary.

Auto Levels Adjusts the overall contrast of an image and may affect its color. If your image needs more contrast and it has a color cast, try this command. Auto Levels works by individually mapping the lightest and darkest pixels in each color channel to black and white.

Auto Contrast Adjusts the overall contrast of an image without affecting its color. Use when your image needs more contrast, but the colors look right. Auto Contrast maps the lightest and darkest pixels in the image to white and black, which makes highlights appear lighter and shadows appear darker.

Auto Color Correction Adjusts the contrast and color by identifying shadows, midtones, and highlights in the image, rather than in individual color channels. It neutralizes the midtones and clips the white and black pixels using a default set of values.

Auto Red Eye Fix Automatically detects and repairs red eyes in an image.

Note: You can use an auto command on an entire image, or you can correct a portion of an image by first making a selection with one of the selection tools.

Adjusting shadows and light

About Levels adjustments

The Levels dialog box is a powerful tonal and color-adjustment tool. You can make levels adjustments on the entire image or a selected portion.

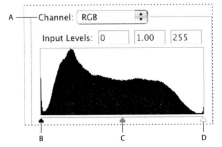

Levels dialog box
A. Channels to adjust color **B.** *Shadow values* **C.** *Highlights value*
D. *Middle tones*

You can do any of the following with the Levels dialog box:

- Set the shadow and highlight values to make sure that your image uses the full tonal range.

- Adjust the brightness of the image's middle tones without affecting the shadow and highlight values.

- Fix a color cast by making grays neutral. You can also enhance an image by adding a slight color cast, for example, by adding a warming effect on a sunset.

- Target shadow and highlight RGB values if you are preparing images for commercial printing.

When you work with Levels, you can work directly on the image pixels or through an adjustment layer. Adjustment layers give you flexibility in the following ways:

- You can modify an adjustment at any time by double-clicking the adjustment layer to reopen the Levels dialog box.

- You can reduce the effect of an adjustment by lowering the adjustment layer's opacity in the Layers palette.

- You can stack adjustment layers to make multiple adjustments and not degrade the image because of too many successive adjustments.

- You can use the adjustment layer's layer mask to confine an adjustment to a portion of your image.

For information on setting press target values for commercial printing, see Help.

To improve shadow and highlight detail

1 In the Editor, choose Enhance > Adjust Lighting > Shadow/Highlights.

2 Drag any of the adjustment sliders or enter values in the text boxes:

Lighten Shadows Brightens the dark areas of your photo and reveals more of the shadow detail that was captured in your image.

Darken Highlights Darkens the light areas of your photo and reveals more of the highlight detail that was captured in your image. Pure white areas of your photo don't have any detail and aren't affected by this adjustment.

Midtone Contrast Adds or reduces the contrast of the middle tones. Use this slider if the image contrast doesn't look right after you've adjusted shadows and highlights.

3 Click OK to accept the adjustments.

You can reset the image to how it looked when you opened the dialog box by holding down Option and clicking the Reset button.

See Figure 8-2 in the color section.

To adjust brightness and contrast in selected areas

The Brightness/Contrast command is best used on selected portions of an image. Use this command to adjust the brightness of an entire image or to reduce contrast results in an image that doesn't use the entire available tonal range. The Levels and Shadow/Highlight commands are better choices for making tonal adjustments.

1 Do one of the following in the Editor:

- Choose Enhance > Adjust Lighting > Brightness/Contrast to make adjustments directly on image pixels.

- Choose Layer > New Adjustment Layer > Brightness/Contrast to make adjustments on a layer.

2 Drag the sliders to adjust the brightness and contrast.

Dragging to the left decreases the level; dragging to the right increases it. The number at the right of each slider displays the brightness or contrast value. Values range from -100 to +100.

3 Click OK.

To quickly lighten or darken isolated areas

The Dodge tool and the Burn tool lighten or darken areas of the image. You can use the Dodge tool to bring out details in shadows and the Burn tool to bring out details in highlights.

See Figure 8-3 in the color section.

1 In the Editor, select the Dodge tool 🔍 or the Burn tool ✋ .

2 Set tool options in the options bar:

Brushes pop-up menu Sets the brush tip. Click the arrow next to the brush sample, choose a brush category from the Brushes pop-up menu, and then select a brush thumbnail.

Size Sets the size of the brush, in pixels. Drag the Size slider or enter a size in the text box.

Range Sets the image tonal range that the tool adjusts. Select Midtones to change the middle range of grays, Shadows to change the dark areas, and Highlights to change the light areas.

Exposure Sets the effect of the tool with each stroke. A higher percentage increases the effect.

💡 *To dodge or burn an area gradually, set the tool with a low exposure value and drag several times over the area you want to correct.*

3 Drag over the part of the image you want to modify.

Correcting color casts

To correct color casts by comparing variations of an image

You can make color and tonal adjustments in the Color Variations dialog box by comparing and choosing different thumbnail variations of the photo. Color Variations works best for average tone images that don't require precise color adjustments.

Note: You can't use the Color Variations command with images in Indexed Color mode.

See Figure 8-4 in the color section.

1 In the Editor, choose Enhance > Adjust Color > Color Variations.

The two preview images show the original image (Before) and the adjusted image after you've made changes.

2 Select an option to choose what you want to adjust in the image:

Shadows, Midtones, or Highlights Specify which part of the tonal range to adjust: dark, middle, or light areas.

Saturation Makes the image colors more vivid (more saturation) or muted (less saturation).

3 Set the amount, or intensity, of each adjustment using the Adjust Color slider. Dragging the slider to the left decreases the amount, and dragging to the right increases it.

4 If you are adjusting the color of midtones, shadows, or highlights, do either of the following:

- To add a color to the image, click the corresponding Increase color thumbnail.

- To subtract a color, click the corresponding Decrease color thumbnail.

Each time you click a thumbnail, all thumbnails are updated.

5 If you are adjusting color saturation, click either the Less Saturation or More Saturation buttons.

6 To undo or redo adjustments, do any of the following:

- Click Reset Image to start over and undo all adjustments.

- Click Undo once or multiple times for each successive adjustment you want to undo. You cannot undo the Reset Image option.

- After undoing a new adjustment, click Redo once or multiple times for each adjustment you want to redo.

7 To apply the adjustments to your image, click OK.

To remove a color cast automatically

A color cast is an unpleasant color shift in a photo. For example, a photo taken indoors without a camera flash may have too much yellow. The Color Cast command changes the overall mixture of colors to remove color casts in an image.

See Figure 8-5 in the color section.

1 In the Editor, choose Enhance > Adjust Color > Remove Color Cast.

2 In your image, click an area that should be white, black, or neutral gray. The image changes based on the color you selected.

3 To start over, and undo the changes made to the image, click the Reset button.

4 Click OK to accept the color change.

For information on removing color casts using Levels, see Help.

Adjusting color saturation and hue

Adjusting saturation and hue

The Hue/Saturation command adjusts the hue (color), saturation (purity), and lightness of the entire image or of individual color components in an image.

Use the Hue slider for special effects, to color a black and white image (like a sepia effect), or to change the color of a portion of an image.

See Figure 8-6 in the color section.

Use the Saturation slider to make colors more vivid or more muted. A good use of this adjustment would be to add a color punch to a landscape by adding saturation to all the colors, or to tone down a distracting color, like a vivid red sweater in a portrait.

See Figure 8-7 in the color section.

Use the Lightness slider in conjunction with the other adjustments to lighten or darken a portion of an image. Take care not to use it on an entire image—this adjustment reduces the overall tonal range.

To change color saturation or hue

1 Do one of the following in the Editor:

- Choose Enhance > Adjust Color > Adjust Hue/Saturation.

• Choose Layer > New Adjustment Layer > Hue/Saturation, or open an existing Hue/Saturation adjustment layer.

The two color bars in the dialog box represent the colors in their order on the color wheel. The upper bar shows the color before the adjustment; the lower bar shows how the adjustment affects all hues at full saturation.

2 In the Edit pop-up menu, choose which colors to adjust:

• Choose Master to adjust all colors at once.

• Choose one of the other preset color ranges listed for the color you want to adjust. An adjustment slider appears between the color bars, which you can use to edit any range of hues. (See "To modify the range of Hue/Saturation sliders" in Help.)

3 For Hue, enter a value or drag the slider until the colors appear as you want.

The values displayed in the text box reflect the number of degrees of rotation around the wheel from the pixel's original color. A positive value indicates clockwise rotation, a negative value counterclockwise rotation. Values range from -180 to +180.

4 For Saturation, enter a value or drag the slider to the right to increase the saturation or to the left to decrease it. Values range from -100 to +100.

5 For Lightness, enter a value or drag the slider to the right to increase the lightness or to the left to decrease it. Values range from -100 to +100. Use care when using this slider on an entire image. It will reduce the tonal range of the overall image.

6 Click OK.

For more information on adjusting the saturation and hue, see Help.

To adjust the color of skin tone

The Adjust Color For Skin Tone command adjusts the overall color in a photo to bring out more natural skin tones. When you click on an area of skin in the photo, Photoshop Elements adjusts the skin tone—as well as all other colors in the photo. You can manually adjust the brown and red colors separately to achieve the final color you want.

See Figure 8-8 in the color section.

1 Open the photo in the Editor, and select the layer that needs correction.

2 Choose Enhance > Adjust Color > Adjust Color For Skin Tone.

3 When the Adjust Skin Tone dialog box appears, click an area of skin.

Photoshop Elements automatically adjusts the colors in the image. Changes might be subtle.

Note: Make sure Preview is selected so that you can see the color changes as they occur.

4 (Optional) Drag any of the following sliders to fine-tune the correction:

Tan Increases or decreases the level of brown in skin tones.

Blush Increases or decreases the level of red in skin tones.

Temperature Changes the overall color of skin tones.

5 When you're finished, click OK. To cancel your changes and start over again, click Reset.

Chapter 9: Cropping and resizing photos

Cropping

To crop an image

The Crop tool removes the part of an image surrounding the crop marquee, or selection. Cropping is useful when you want to remove distracting background elements and focus in on the target of your photo. By default, when you crop a photo, the resolution remains the same as the original photo. If you use a preset size, the resolution changes to fit the preset.

Crop a photo to remove some of the distracting background.

1 In the Editor, select the Crop tool 耳 .

2 If you want to use a resolution other than that of the original photo, select one of the following options from the Aspect Ratio menu or specify new custom values in the Width and Height boxes in the options bar:

No Restriction Lets you resize the image to any dimension.

Photo Ratio Retains the original aspect ratio of the photo when you crop. The Width and Height boxes show the values that are used for the cropped image.

Preset size Specifies a preset size for the cropped photo. If you want your final output to be a specific size, such as 4 x 6 to fit a picture frame, choose that preset size.

Note: When you specify values for the Width and Height boxes, the Aspect Ratio menu changes to Custom.

3 Drag over the part of the image you want to keep. When you release the mouse button, the crop marquee appears as a bounding box with handles at the corners and sides.

4 (Optional) Adjust the crop marquee by doing any of the following:

• To move the marquee to another position, place the pointer inside the bounding box, and drag.

• To resize the marquee, drag a handle. (If you choose No Restriction from the Aspect Ratio menu, you can constrain the proportions while scaling by holding down Shift as you drag a corner handle.)

• To rotate the marquee, position the pointer outside the bounding box (the pointer turns into a curved arrow ⤴), and drag. (You can't rotate the crop marquee for an image in Bitmap mode.)

Note: You can change the color and opacity of the crop shield (the cropped area surrounding the image) in the options bar.

5 Click the Commit button ✔ located in the options bar, or press Return to finish the cropping. If you want to cancel the cropping operation, click the Cancel button ⊘ or press Esc.

Click the Commit button to accept a crop.

For more information, see "To resample an image" on page 83.

To crop to a selection boundary

Using the Crop command, you can remove the areas that fall outside of the current selection. When you crop to a selection boundary, Photoshop Elements trims the image to the bounding box that contains the selection. (Irregularly shaped selections, such as those made by using the Lasso tool, are cropped to a rectangular bounding box that contains the selection.) If you use the Crop command without first making a selection, Photoshop Elements automatically centers a crop bounding box 50 pixels from each edge.

1 In the Editor, use any selection tool, such as the Rectangular Marquee tool ⬚, to select the part of the image you want to keep.

2 Choose Image > Crop.

To use the Cookie Cutter tool

The Cookie Cutter tool crops a photo into a shape that you choose. After you drag the shape in your photo, you can move and resize the bounding box until you have just the area you want.

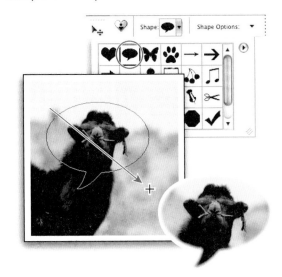

Use the Cookie Cutter tool to clip a photo into a fun shape.

1 In the Editor, select the Cookie Cutter tool 💟.

2 Click the Shapes menu on the options bar to view a library of shapes from which to choose. To view other libraries, click the triangle on the right side of the currently open library and choose a new library from the list that appears.

3 Click a shape to select it.

4 Click the Shape Options arrow to display the Cookie Cutter Options window. Set any of the following Shape Options:

Unconstrained Draws the shape to any size or dimension you'd like.

Defined Proportions Keeps the height and width of the cropped shape in proportion.

Defined Size Crops the photo to the exact size of the shape you chose.

Fixed Size Specifies exact measurements for the finished shape.

From Center Draws the shape from the center.

5 Enter a value for Feather to soften the edges of the finished shape.

Note: Feathering softens the edges of the cropped image so that the edges fade out and blend in with the background.

6 Choose Crop to crop the image to the shape.

7 Drag in the image to create the shape boundary and move it into the desired location on the image.

8 Click the Commit button ✔ located in the options bar, or press Return to finish the cropping. If you want to cancel the cropping operation, click the Cancel button ⊘ or press Esc.

To change the size of the canvas

You can add space to one or all sides of an image. Added canvas appears in the currently selected background color on the Background layer; in other layers, the added canvas is transparent. In the new canvas space, you can add text or resize your photo to fit.

Increasing the size of the canvas makes room for a colored border.

1 In the Editor, choose Image > Resize > Canvas Size.

2 Do one of the following:

• In the Width and Height boxes, enter the full dimensions of the new canvas in the Width and Height boxes. Choose the units of measurement you want. The Columns option measures width in terms of the columns specified in the Units & Rulers preferences.

- Select Relative, and enter the amount by which you want to increase or decrease the size of the canvas. Enter a negative number to decrease the size of the canvas. Use this option if you want to increase the canvas by a specified amount, such as 2 inches on each side.

3 For Anchor, click a square to indicate where to position the existing image on the new canvas.

4 To change the color of the added canvas, choose an option from the Canvas Extension Color menu.

5 Click OK.

To straighten an image

1 In the Editor, select the Straighten tool .

2 To straighten all of the layers in the image, select Rotate All Layers, and then choose an option from the Canvas Options menu (this menu is available only if you select Rotate All Layers):

Grow Canvas To Fit Resizes the canvas to fit the rotated image. Straightening causes corners of the image to fall outside of the current canvas. The straightened image will contain areas of blank background, but no pixels will be clipped.

Crop To Remove Background Crops the image to remove any blank background areas that become visible after straightening. Some pixels will be clipped.

Crop To Original Size Keeps the canvas the same size as the original image. The straightened image will include areas of blank background and some pixels will be clipped.

Straightening and cropping to remove the background

3 Do one of the following to straighten the image:

- To align horizontally, draw a line in the image to represent the new straight horizontal edge.
- To align vertically, hold down Command and draw a line to represent the new straight vertical edge.

To automatically straighten an image

- To automatically straighten the image and leave the canvas around the image, choose Image > Rotate > Straighten Image. The straightened image will contain areas of blank background, but no pixels will be clipped.
- To automatically straighten and crop the image, choose Image > Rotate > Straighten And Crop Image. The straightened image will not contain areas of blank background, but some pixels will be clipped.

To divide a scanned image containing multiple photos

If you scanned several pictures at once on a flatbed scanner, you can automatically divide and straighten the scanned image into its component photos. The photos must have a clear separation between them.

Separating images scanned from one page into three separate images.

❖ In the Editor, choose Image > Divide Scanned Photos. Photoshop Elements automatically divides the image and places each photo in a separate file.

💡 *For images with white around the border (images of light skies, snow, and so on) this command works best if you cover the image on the scanner with a piece of dark paper.*

Image size and resolution

About image size and resolution

The image size (or pixel dimensions) of an image is a measure of the number of pixels along an image's width and height. For example, your digital camera may take a photo that is 1024 pixels wide and 768

pixels high. These two measurements have a direct correlation to the image's file size, and both are an indication of the amount of image data in a photo.

Resolution is the fineness of detail you can see in an image. It is measured in pixels per inch (ppi). The more pixels per inch, the greater the resolution. Generally, the higher the resolution of your image, the better the printed image quality.

Although a digital image contains a specific amount of image data, it doesn't have a specific physical output size or resolution. As you change the resolution of a file, its physical dimensions change, and as you change the width or height of an image, its resolution changes.

You can see the relationship between image size and resolution in the Image Size dialog box (choose Image > Resize > Image Size). Deselect Resample Image, because you don't want to change the amount of image data in your photo. Then change the width or the height or the resolution. As you change one value, the other two values change accordingly.

Same image printed at 72-ppi and 300-ppi; inset zoom 200%

If you need to print using a specific resolution, or if you want to print an image significantly smaller or larger than the image's pixel dimensions allow, you can resample the image. Resampling involves either throwing away or adding pixels to the image to achieve the desired dimensions or resolution.

About printer resolution

Printer resolution is measured in ink dots per inch, also known as dpi. Generally, the more dots per inch, the finer the printed output you'll get. Most inkjet printers have a resolution of 720 to 2880 dpi.

Printer resolution is different from, but related to image resolution. To print a high quality photo on an inkjet printer, an image resolution of about 220 ppi should provide good results. Using a lower resolution you can print a slightly larger photo—if you are willing to accept some image degradation. You'll see a warning if you chose a print size that causes the photo to print at less than 220 ppi.

About monitor resolution

Your monitor's resolution is described in pixel dimensions. For example, if your monitor resolution is set to 1024 x 768 and your photo's pixel dimensions are the same size, at 100% the photo will fill the screen. How large an image appears on-screen depends on a combination of factors—the pixel dimensions of the image, the monitor size, and the monitor resolution setting. In Photoshop Elements, you can change the image magnification on-screen, so you can easily work with images of any pixel dimensions.

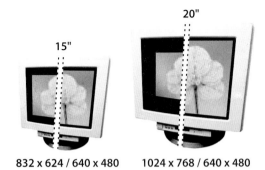

832 x 624 / 640 x 480   1024 x 768 / 640 x 480

A 620- by 400-pixel image displayed on monitors of various sizes and resolutions.

When preparing images for viewing on-screen, you should consider the lowest monitor resolution that your photo is likely to be viewed on.

To display the image size of an open file

❖ In the Editor, click the file information box at the bottom of the document, and hold down the mouse button. The box displays the width and height of the image (both in pixels and in the unit of measurement currently selected for the rulers), the number of channels, and the image resolution.

To view the print size on-screen

❖ Do one of the following in the Editor:

• Choose View > Print Size.

• Select the Hand tool or Zoom tool, and click Print Size in the options bar.

The magnification of the image is adjusted to display its approximate printed size, as specified in the Document Size section of the Image Size dialog box. Keep in mind that the size and resolution of your monitor affect the on-screen print size.

To change the print dimensions and resolution of an image

You can change the physical printed size and resolution of an image without resampling. You might need to do this if you are sending the image to a print shop that requires files be at a specific resolution.

If you are printing directly from Photoshop Elements, you don't have to perform this procedure. Instead, you can choose a size in the Print dialog box and Photoshop Elements applies the appropriate image resolution.

Note: If you want to change only the print dimensions or the resolution and adjust the total number of pixels in the image proportionately, you must resample the image. (See "To resample an image" on page 83.)

1 In the Editor, choose Image > Resize > Image Size.

2 Make sure that Resample Image is deselected. When deselected, you can change the print dimensions and resolution without changing the total number of pixels in the image.

3 To maintain the current proportions of image width to image height, select Constrain Proportions. This option automatically updates the width as you change the height, and vice versa.

4 Under Document Size, enter new values for the height and width. If desired, choose a new unit of measurement. Note that for Width, the Columns

option uses the width and gutter sizes specified in the Units & Rulers preferences.

5 For Resolution, enter a new value. If desired, choose a new unit of measurement.

6 Click OK.

To return to the original values displayed in the Image Size dialog box, hold down Option and click Reset.

To resample an image

Changing the pixel dimensions of an image is called *resampling.* Resampling affects not only the size of an image on-screen but also its image quality and its printed output—either its printed dimensions or its image resolution. Resampling can degrade image quality. When you *downsample,* meaning that you decrease the number of pixels in your image, information is deleted from the image. When you *resample up,* or increase the number of pixels in your image, new pixels are added based on color values of existing pixels, and the image loses some detail and sharpness.

Resampling an image
A. *Image resampled down* **B.** *Original image* **C.** *Image resampled up*

To avoid the need for resampling up, scan or create the image at the resolution required for your printer or output device. If you want to preview the effects of changing pixel dimensions on-screen or print proofs at different resolutions, resample a duplicate of your file.

If you're preparing images for the web, it's useful to specify image size in terms of the pixel dimensions.

1 In the Editor, choose Image > Resize > Image Size.

2 Select Resample Image, and choose an interpolation method:

Nearest Neighbor Fast but less precise method. This method is recommended for use with illustrations containing edges that are not anti-aliased, to preserve hard edges and produce a smaller file. However, this method can create jagged edges, which become apparent when distorting or scaling an image or performing multiple manipulations on a selection.

Bilinear Medium-quality method.

Bicubic Slow but more precise method, resulting in the smoothest tonal gradations.

Bicubic Smoother Use when you're enlarging images.

Bicubic Sharper Use for reducing the size of an image. This method maintains the detail in a resampled image. It may, however, oversharpen some areas of an image. In this case, try using Bicubic.

3 To maintain the current proportions of pixel width to pixel height, select Constrain Proportions. This option automatically updates the width as you change the height, and vice versa.

4 In Pixel Dimensions, enter values for Width and Height. To enter values as percentages of the current dimensions, choose Percent as the unit of measurement.

The new file size for the image appears at the top of the Image Size dialog box, with the old file size in parentheses.

5 Click OK to change the pixel dimensions and resample the image.

For best results in producing a smaller image, downsample and apply the Unsharp Mask filter. To produce a larger image, rescan the image at a higher resolution.

Chapter 10: Retouching and transforming

Retouching

To remove red eye

The Red Eye Removal tool removes red eye in flash photos of people.

Red eye is caused by a reflection of the subject's retina by the camera's flash. You'll see it more often when taking pictures in a darkened room because the subject's iris is wide open. To avoid red eye, use the camera's red eye reduction feature, if available.

See Figure 10-1 in the color section.

1 Select the Red Eye Removal tool .

2 Do one of the following:

- Click the Auto button in the options bar. Photoshop Elements automatically identifies and fixes red eyes. If you are not happy with the results, try one of the other options.

- Click a red area of an eye in the image.

- Draw a selection over one red eye.

To remove spots and imperfections

The Spot Healing Brush quickly removes blemishes and other imperfections in your photos. You can either click once on a blemish, or click and drag to smooth away imperfections in an area.

Easily remove spots or imperfections using the Spot Healing Brush tool.

1 In the Editor, select the Spot Healing Brush tool .

2 Choose a brush size. A brush that is slightly larger than the area you want to fix works best so that you can cover the entire area with one click.

3 Choose a Type option in the options bar.

Proximity Match Uses the pixels around the edge of the selection to find an image area to use as a patch for the selected area. If this option doesn't provide a satisfactory fix, undo the fix and try the Create Texture option.

Create Texture Uses all the pixels in the selection to create a texture in which to fix the area. If the texture doesn't work, try dragging through the area a second time.

4 Click the area you want to fix in the image, or click and drag over a larger area.

To fix large imperfections

The Healing Brush fixes large areas of imperfections when you drag over them. You can remove objects from a uniform background, such as an object in a field of grass.

Before and after using Healing Brush

1 In the Editor, select the Healing Brush tool ✐.

2 Choose a brush size from the options bar and set healing brush options:

Mode Determines how the source or pattern blends with existing pixels. Normal mode lays new pixels over the original pixels. Replace mode preserves film grain and texture at the edges of the brush stroke.

Source Sets the source to use for repairing pixels. Sampled uses pixels from the current image. Pattern uses pixels from the pattern you specify in the Pattern palette.

Aligned Samples pixels continuously without losing the current sampling point, even if you release the mouse button. Deselect Aligned to continue using the

sampled pixels from the initial sampling point each time you stop and resume painting.

Sample All Layers Samples data from all visible layers. Deselect Use All Layers to sample only from the active layer.

3 Position the pointer in any open image and Option-click to sample data.

Note: If you are sampling from one image and applying to another, both images must be in the same color mode unless one of the images is in Grayscale mode.

4 Drag in the image over the flaw to meld existing data with sampled data. The sampled pixels are melded with the existing pixels each time you release the mouse button.

💡 *If there is a strong contrast at the edges of the area you want to heal, make a selection before you use the Healing Brush tool. The selection should be bigger than the area you want to heal but should precisely follow the boundary of contrasting pixels. When you paint with the Healing Brush tool, the selection prevents colors from bleeding in from the outside.*

To clone images or areas on an image

The Clone Stamp tool paints with a sample of an image, which you can use to duplicate objects, remove image imperfections, or paint over objects in your photo.

Original photos (top), after adding two starfish with the Clone Stamp tool (center), and after removing a person with the Clone Stamp tool (bottom)

1 In the Editor, select the Clone Stamp tool ⊥.

2 (Optional) Set options in the options bar:

Brushes pop-up menu Sets the brush tip. Click the arrow next to the brush sample, choose a brush category from the Brushes pop-up menu, and then select a brush thumbnail.

Size Sets the size of the brush in pixels. Drag the Size pop-up slider or enter a size in the text box.

Mode Determines how the source or pattern blends with existing pixels. Normal mode lays new pixels over the original pixels. Replace mode preserves film grain and texture at the edges of the brush stroke.

Opacity Sets the opacity of the paint you apply. A low opacity setting allows pixels under a paint stroke to show through. Drag the pop-up slider or enter an opacity value.

Aligned Moves the sampled area with the cursor as you begin to paint, regardless of how many times you stop and resume painting. Selecting this option is useful when you want to eliminate unwanted areas such as a telephone line across the skyline or a rip in a scanned photo. If Aligned is deselected, the Clone Stamp tool applies the sampled area from the initial sampling point each time you stop and resume painting. Deselecting this option is useful for applying multiple copies of the same part of an image to different areas within the same image or to another image.

Sample All Layers To sample (copy) data from all visible layers, select Use All Layers. To sample data from only the active layer, deselect this option.

3 Position the pointer on the part of any open image you want to sample, and Option-click. The tool duplicates the pixels at this sample point in your image as you paint.

4 Drag to paint with the tool.

For information on replacing colors, blurring, or sharpening, search for these topics in Help.

Transforming

To rotate or flip an item

You can rotate or flip a selection, a layer, or an entire image. Make sure to choose the correction command depending on the item you want to rotate or flip.

1 In the Editor, select the photo, layer, selection, or shape you want to rotate or flip.

2 Choose Image > Rotate, and choose one of the following commands from the submenu:

90˚ Left, Layer 90˚ Left, and Selection 90˚ Left Rotate the photo, layer, or selection a quarter-turn counterclockwise. (Rotate Selection is only available when you have an active selection in an image.)

90˚ Right, Layer 90˚ Right, and Selection 90˚ Right Rotate the photo, layer, or selection a quarter-turn clockwise.

180˚, Layer 180˚, and Selection 180˚ Rotate the photo, layer, or selection a half-turn.

Custom Rotates the item by the amount you specify. If you select this option, enter the number of degrees you want to rotate the item by, and the direction in which you want to rotate the item. Then click OK.

Flip Horizontal, Flip Layer Horizontal, and Flip Selection Horizontal Flip the photo, layer, or selection horizontally.

Flip Vertical, Flip Layer Vertical, and Flip Selection Vertical Flip the photo, layer, or selection vertically.

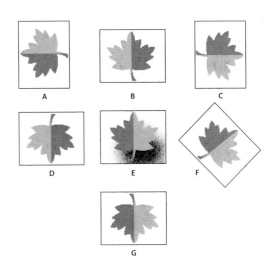

Rotating an image
A. Rotate 90˚ left **B.** *Flip Horizontal* **C.** *Rotate 90˚ right*
D. *Rotate 180˚* **E.** *Original image* **F.** *Free rotate* **G.** *Flip Vertical*

To freely rotate an item

With the Free Rotate Layer and Free Rotate Selection commands, you can rotate an item by any amount.

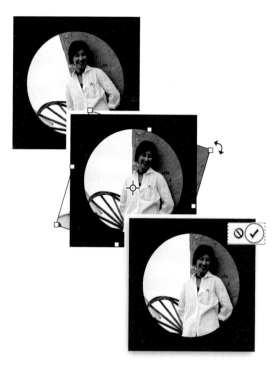

Using the Free Rotate Layer command to straighten image and clicking the Commit button to apply the rotation.

1 In the Editor, select the layer or selection you want to rotate.

2 Choose Image > Rotate > Free Rotate Layer or Selection. A bounding box appears in the image.

Note: *If you select an image that is a background layer (such as a photo imported from a camera or scanner), you are given the option of turning it into a regular layer so that you can transform it.*

3 (Optional) To change the point around which the item rotates, click a square on the reference point locator ▦ in the options bar.

4 Do one of the following to specify the rotation amount:

• Move the pointer outside of the bounding border until it becomes a curved, two-sided arrow ↰↴, and then drag. To constrain the rotation to 15° increments, hold down Shift as you drag.

• Type an angle of rotation between -180 (maximum counterclockwise rotation) and 180 (maximum clockwise rotation) in the angle degree △ text box of the options bar. The further you click from the bounding box, the more control you have over the angle.

5 Do one of the following:

• To apply the transformation, double-click inside the bounding box, click the Commit button ✔ , or press Return.

• To cancel the transformation, click the Cancel button ◌ , or press Esc.

To freely transform an item

The Free Transform command lets you apply transformations (rotating, scaling, skewing, distorting, and perspective) in one step. Instead of choosing different commands, you simply hold down a key on your keyboard to switch between transformation types.

1 In the Editor, select the item you want to transform.

2 Choose Image > Transform > Free Transform. If you are transforming a shape, choose Image > Transform Shape > Free Transform Shape.

Note: *If you select a photo that is a background layer (such as a photo imported from a camera or scanner), you are given the option of turning it into a regular layer so that you can transform it.*

3 (Optional) To change the point around which the item rotates, click a square on the reference point locator ⊞ in the options bar.

4 Do one or more of the following to transform the object:

- To scale, drag any handle on the bounding box. To scale the width and height proportionally, either press Shift as you drag a corner handle, or click the Maintain Aspect Ratio button ⬚ in the options bar and then drag a corner handle.

- To rotate, move the pointer outside of the bounding box and drag. When positioned outside the bounding box, the pointer becomes a curved, two-sided arrow ↰. Press Shift and drag to constrain the rotation to 15° increments.

- To distort, press Command, and drag any handle. When positioned over a handle, the pointer becomes a gray arrowhead ◤.

- To skew, press Command+Shift and drag a handle in the middle of a side of the bounding box. When positioned over a side handle, the pointer becomes a gray arrowhead with a small double arrow ◤↔.

- To apply perspective, press Command+Option+Shift, and drag a corner handle. When positioned over a corner handle, the pointer becomes a gray arrowhead ◤.

  To undo the last handle adjustment, choose Edit > Undo.

5 Do one of the following:

- To commit the transformation, double-click inside the bounding box, click the Commit button ✔, or press Return.

- To cancel the transformation, click the Cancel button ⊘, or press Esc.

  For information about scaling, distorting, applying perspective, or transforming in 3D, search for these topics in Help.

To apply a transformation to the Background layer

Before you can apply transformations to the Background layer, you need to convert it to a regular layer.

1 In the Editor, select the Background layer in the Layers palette.

2 Convert the Background. (See "To convert the Background layer to a regular layer" on page 49.)

3 Apply the transformation.

Chapter 11: Using filters, effects, and styles

Filters, effects, and layer styles

About filters, effects, and layer styles

Filters let you change the look of your images, for instance giving them the appearance of impressionistic paintings or mosaic tiles, or adding unique lighting or distortions.

In addition to filters, Photoshop Elements also provides a variety of effects—such as shadows, glows, bevels, overlays, and strokes—that let you quickly change the appearance of a layer's contents. Effects differ from filters in that when you move or edit the contents of the layer, effects change accordingly. For example, if you apply a drop shadow effect to a text layer, the shadow changes automatically when you edit the text.

Layer styles let you quickly apply effects to a layer's content. Preset layer styles appear in the Styles palette and can be applied with just a click of the mouse. You can scan through a variety of predefined layer styles and apply a style with just a click of the mouse, or you can create a custom style by applying multiple effects to a layer.

Note: You cannot apply layer effects and styles to a background, a locked layer, or a layer set.

When you add effects styles, or both to a layer, an "f" icon appears to the right of the layer's name in the Layers palette. You can view the effects and layer styles used in a layer by clicking the triangle next to the "f" icon. If you double-click a style or effect in the Layers palette, you can edit the effect or the shadow distance, glow size, and bevel size of layer style.

For more information on using filters, effects, and layer styles, including descriptions for each filter, see Help.

To use the Styles And Effects palette

The Styles And Effects palette (Window > Styles And Effects) displays a thumbnail example of the result of applying a filter, effect, or layer style, to an image. (It's a good idea to preview the specific filter on your photo before taking the time to apply it.) In addition, many filters have specific options that you can access with the palette.

You can combine the different categories of filters, effects, and layer styles to create unique images from a simple photograph. For example, you can create a dramatic look by combining the Outer Glow category from the Layer Styles portion of the palette with Neon Nights from the Image Effect category in the Effects portion of the palette.

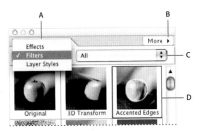

Styles And Effects palette
A. Category menu B. Palette menu C. Library menu D. Selected thumbnail

❖ Do one of the following:

- To view the visual effects by their names, choose List View from the More pop-up menu at the top of the palette. When you select a name, the left side of the palette displays thumbnails with and without the filter or effect.

- To view the visual effects as thumbnails, choose Thumbnail View from the More pop-up menu at the top of the palette.

- To choose whether to display filters, effects, or layer styles, choose one from the Category menu.

- To narrow the display to a specific type of filter, effect, or layer style, choose a type from the Library menu.

Filter Gallery

The Filter Gallery (Filter > Filter Gallery) lets you apply filters cumulatively, and apply individual filters more than once. You can also rearrange filters and change the settings of each filter you've applied to achieve the effect you want. Because you can apply more than one filter to an image when you use the Filter Gallery dialog box, you have a lot of control over

the way your image is affected by each filter. The Filter Gallery is often the best choice for applying filters because it's flexible and easy to use.

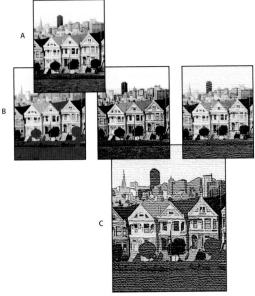

Applying filters through the Filters Gallery
A. Original photo B. Photos each with a single filter applied
C. Three filters applied cumulatively

However, not all filters are available from the Filter Gallery. Some are available only as individual commands from the Filter menu or from the Styles And Effects palette. Also, you cannot apply effects and layer styles from the Filter Gallery, as you can from the Styles And Effects palette.

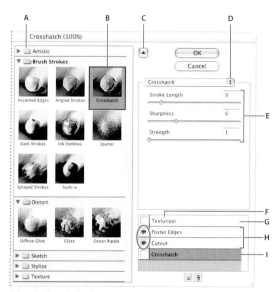

Filter Gallery dialog box
A. Filter category B. Thumbnail of selected filter C. Show/Hide filter thumbnails D. Filters pop-up menu E. Options for selected filter F. List of filter effects to apply or arrange G. Hidden filter H. Filters applied cumulatively but not selected I. Filter selected but not applied

Chapter 12: Painting

Painting overview

About painting

The Standard Edit workspace in Photoshop Elements provides a variety of tools for applying and editing color. When you select a painting tool, the option bar displays a variety of preset brush tips and settings for brush size, paint blending, opacity, and airbrush effects. You can create new brush presets and save them in brush libraries. You can customize the brush and settings for any of the painting and editing tools and manage them using the Preset Manager.

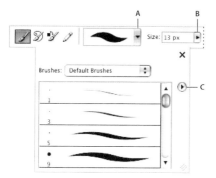

Brush options in options bar.
A. Brush pop-up palette and brush thumbnail *B.* Brush size pop-up slider and text box *C.* Palette menu button

The Brush tool paints smooth, antialiased lines. Other painting tools include the Pencil tool for making hard edged lines and the eraser tools for applying the background color or erasing color pixels on layers. The Paint Bucket tool and Fill command fill areas of your image with color or patterns. The Pattern Stamp tool paints with one of the predefined patterns or a pattern that you design. The Impressionist Brush tool affects existing color by applying stylized brush strokes. The Smudge tool also affects existing image colors by simulating the action of dragging a finger through wet paint.

You can learn more about painting, painting tools, patterns, and gradients in Help.

About foreground and background colors

You apply the foreground color when you paint with the Brush or Pencil tools, and when you fill selections with the Paint Bucket tool. The color you apply to the Background layer with the Eraser tool is called the background color. You can see and change the foreground and background colors in the two overlapping boxes at the bottom of the toolbox. The top box is the foreground color, and the bottom box is the background color. The foreground and background colors are also used together by the Gradient tool and some special effects filters.

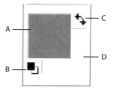

Foreground and background color boxes in toolbox
A. Foreground color box *B.* Click to use default colors (black and white) *C.* Click to switch the foreground and background colors *D.* Background color box

You can change the foreground or background color in the toolbox by using the eyedropper, the Color Swatches palette, or the Adobe Color Picker.

For more information about choosing colors and using blending modes, see Help.

Chapter 13: Adding text and shapes

Adding and editing text

About text

In the Editor, you use the Horizontal Type and Vertical Type tools to create and edit text. The new text you type is entered on a new type layer. You can create single-line text or paragraph text. Each line of single line text you enter is independent—the length of a line grows or shrinks as you edit it, but it doesn't wrap to the next line. To create a new line of text, press Enter. Paragraph text wraps within the paragraph boundaries you specify.

Single-line text (top of image) and paragraph text (bottom of image).

You can use the type mask tools to create a selection in the shape of text. You can then create different effects and cut-outs with the text.

Clicking in an image with a type tool puts the tool in edit mode so you can enter and edit text. You must commit changes to the type before you can perform other operations, like selecting menu commands. To determine if the type tool is in edit mode, look in the options bar. If you see the Commit button ✔ and Cancel button ⊘, the type tool is in edit mode.

Note: When you add text to an image that's in Index Color mode, Photoshop Elements does not create a new text layer. The text you type appears as masked text.

For information on adding and editing text, including Asian type, see Help.

Creating shapes

About shapes

In Photoshop Elements, shapes are vector graphics, which means they are made up of lines and curves defined by their geometric characteristics instead of pixels. Vector graphics are resolution-independent—that is, they can be scaled to any size and printed at any resolution without losing detail or clarity. You can move, resize, or change them without losing the quality of the graphic. Because computer monitors display images on a pixel grid, vector data is displayed as pixels on-screen.

Shapes are created in shape layers. A shape layer can contain a single shape or multiple shapes, depending on the shape area option you select. You can choose to have more than one shape in a layer.

You can change the color of a shape by editing its fill layer and applying layer styles to it. The shape tools provide an easy way to create buttons, navigation bars, and other items used on web pages.

Vector objects created with the shape tools in Photoshop Elements

For information on adding and editing shapes, see Help.

Chapter 14: Printing and sharing photos

Printing photos

To print a photo

Before you print your photos, you need to let Photoshop Elements know some basic information about your print job, such as the size of paper you are using and the page orientation. Set these options in the Page Setup dialog box. You might also need to specify measurement units in the Preferences dialog box.

1 Open the photo you want print.

2 Click the Print button 🖶 in the shortcuts bar or choose File > Print).

3 Set the options you want in the Print Preview dialog box. (See "Print Preview options" in Help.)

4 To change the page printing options, click Page Setup. Photoshop Elements uses these options each time you print, until you change them. (These settings only apply to printing in the Editor.)

💡 *If you're using more than one printer at home, you'll need to go through the setup options each time you change printers.*

5 Click Print and set the options for your printer in the Print dialog box that appears. These options vary according to your printer's driver.

6 Click Print.

💡 *If your photos are not printing at a particular size, try resizing the photo to the specific dimensions you want before you print. (See "To change the print dimensions and resolution of an image" on page 83.)*

To create a contact sheet

Contact sheets let you easily preview and catalog groups of images by displaying a series of thumbnails on a single page. You can automatically create and place thumbnails on a page using the Contact Sheet II command.

1 Do one of the following:

- (Photoshop Elements) Choose File > Contact Sheet II.

- (Bridge) Select a folder of images or specific image files. From the Bridge menu, choose Tools > Photoshop Elements > Contact Sheet II. Unless you select specific images, the contact sheet will include all the images currently displayed in Adobe Bridge. You can select a different image folder or select other currently open images after the Contact Sheet II dialog box opens.

Note: Click to select an image in Bridge. Shift-click to select a series of images, or Command-click to select noncontiguous images.

2 In the Contact Sheet II dialog box, specify the images to use by choosing one of the following from the Use menu in the Source Images area:

Current Open Documents Uses any image that is currently open in Photoshop Elements.

Folder Lets you click Choose to specify the folder containing the images you want to use. Select Include All Subfolders to include images inside any subfolders.

Selected Images From Bridge Uses images displayed in Bridge. All images in Bridge are used unless you select specific images before choosing the Contact

Sheet II command. Images in subfolders are not included.

3 In the Document area, specify the dimensions, resolution, and color mode for the contact sheet. Select Flatten All Layers to create a contact sheet with all images and text on a single layer. Deselect Flatten All Layers to create a contact sheet in which each image is on a separate layer and each caption is on a separate text layer.

4 In the Thumbnails area, specify layout options for the thumbnail previews.

- For Place, choose whether to arrange thumbnails across first (from left to right, then top to bottom) or down first (from top to bottom, then left to right).

- Enter the number of columns and rows that you want per contact sheet. The maximum dimensions for each thumbnail are displayed to the right, along with a visual preview of the specified layout.

- Select Use Auto-Spacing to let Photoshop Elements automatically space the thumbnails in the contact sheet. If you deselect Use Auto-Spacing, you can specify the vertical and horizontal space around the thumbnails. The contact sheet preview in the dialog box is automatically updated as you specify the spacing.

- Select Rotate For Best Fit to rotate the images, regardless of their orientation, so they fit efficiently on a contact sheet.

When Rotate For Best Fit is deselected, thumbnails appear in their correct orientation (left). When it is selected, the pictures are rotated to achieve the best fit (right).

5 Select Use Filename As Caption to label the thumbnails using their source image file names. Use the menu to specify a caption font and font size.

6 Click OK.

To create a picture package

With the Picture Package command, you can place multiple copies of images on a single page, much as portrait studios do with school photos and other photo packages. You can choose from a variety of size and placement options to customize your package layout.

1 Do one of the following:

- (Photoshop Elements) Choose File > Picture Package. If you have multiple images open, Picture Package uses the frontmost image.

- (Bridge) Select one ore more photos and then choose Tools > Photoshop Elements > Picture Package. (The Picture Package command uses the first image listed in Bridge unless you select a specific image before giving the Picture Package command.)

If you're using only the frontmost image or a selected image from Bridge, skip to step 3.

2 Add one or more images to the layout by doing one of the following:

- In the Source Images area of the Picture Package dialog box, choose either File or Folder from the Use menu and click Choose. If you choose Folder, you can select Include All Subfolders to include images inside any subfolders.

- Click a placeholder in the preview layout and browse to select an image.

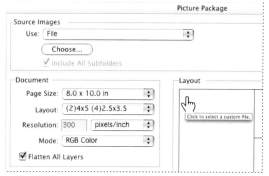

Click a placeholder in the Picture Package preview layout, then browse to select an image.

- Drag an image from the desktop or a folder into a placeholder.

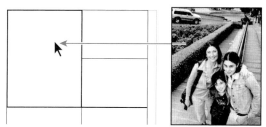

Add an image to a picture package by dragging the image from the desktop into a placeholder.

You can change any image in the layout by clicking a placeholder and browsing to select an image.

3 In the Document area of the Picture Package dialog box, select page size, layout, resolution, and color mode. A thumbnail of the chosen layout appears on the right side of the dialog box. You can also create your own custom layouts.

4 Select Flatten All Layers to create a picture package with all images and label text on a single layer. Deselect Flatten All Layers to create a picture package with separate image layers and text layers (for labels). If you place each image and label on a separate layer, you can update your picture package after it's been saved. However, the layers increase the file size of your picture package.

5 In the Label area, choose the source for label text from the Content menu or choose None. If you choose Custom Text, enter the text for the label in the Custom Text field.

6 Specify font, font size, color, opacity, position, and rotation for the labels.

7 Click OK.

To customize a picture package layout

You can modify existing layouts or create new layouts using the Picture Package Edit Layout feature. Your custom layouts are saved as text files and stored in the Layouts folder in the Presets folder. You can then reuse your saved layouts.

1 Do one of the following:

- (Photoshop Elements) Choose File > Picture Package.

- (Bridge) Choose Tools > Photoshop > Picture Package.

2 In the Picture Package dialog box, choose a layout from the Layout menu if you're creating a layout or customizing an existing one.

3 Click the Edit Layout button.

4 In the Picture Package Edit Layout dialog box, enter a name for the custom layout in the Name text box.

5 (Optional) In the Layout area of the Picture Package Edit Layout dialog box, choose a size from the Page Size menu or enter values in the Width and Height text boxes. You can use the Units menu to specify inches, centimeters, pixels, or millimeters.

6 To add or delete a placeholder, do one of the following:

- Click Add Zone to add a placeholder to the layout.

- Select a placeholder and click Delete Zone to delete it from the layout.

7 To modify a placeholder, select a placeholder and do one of the following:

- Enter values in the Width and Height text boxes to resize a placeholder.

- Click and drag a handle to resize a placeholder. If you resize a rectangle placeholder with an image in it, Picture Package will snap the image within the vertical or horizontal placeholder, depending on the way the zone is being resized.

- Enter values in the X and Y boxes to move a place-holder.

- Enter values in the Position and Size boxes to position and size a placeholder.

- Click and drag a placeholder to the location you want in the layout.

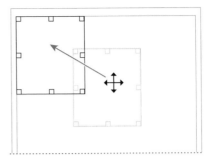

Dragging a placeholder to a new location in the Picture Package layout

8 In the Grid area of the Picture Package Edit Layout dialog box, select the Snap To option to display a grid to help you position the elements in the custom layout. Enter a value in the Size text box to change the appearance of the grid.

9 Click Save.

Tutorials

Figure 2-1

You can easily adjust the lighting in your photos by using Smart Fix in the Quick Fix workspace. Original image (top) and after using Quick Fix (bottom).

Figure 2-2

Use the Adjust Color For Skin Tone command in Standard Edit to bring out natural skin tones in the people in your photos, and enhance the colors throughout the image.

Tutorials (continued)

Figure 2-3

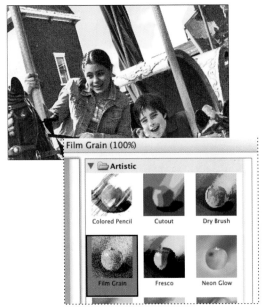

In Standard Edit, you can use filters, such as Film Grain, to create artistic effects.

Figure 2-4

Easily add stylized text to your photos using the Text tool in Standard Edit.

Selecting parts of an image

Figure 7-1

A

B

C

Use the Magic Extractor in Standard Edit to select and remove objects from your photos.
A. Marking the area you want to extract with red dots
B. Marking the background area with blue dots
C. Extracted image

Figure 7-2

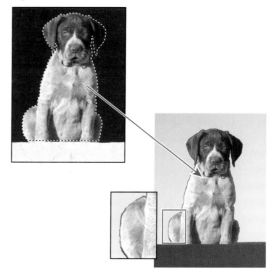
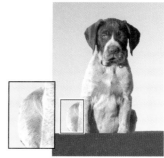

Use the Defringe command in Standard Edit to clean up the pixels around an object that you've copied to a new layer or image. Original photo (top), after copying to a new image (center), and after using the Defringe command (bottom).

Correcting and understanding color

Figure 8-1

Use the Auto Colors palette in the Quick Fix workspace to automatically bring out the natural colors in your photos.

Figure 8-2

Use the Shadows/Highlights command in Standard Edit to soften images and bring out detail behind shadows. Original image (top), and after adjusting shadows and highlights (bottom). Notice the face is softer and more detail is visible behind the sunglasses after the adjustment.

Figure 8-3

Use the Burn tool in Standard Edit to darken specific areas in a photo, such as this sun-bleached background (top center). Use the Dodge tool to lighten specific areas of a photo, such as this woman's face (bottom right). Original image is on the left.

Figure 8-4

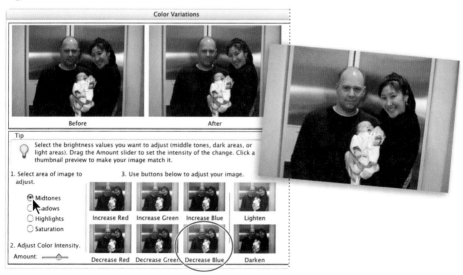

Use the Color Variations dialog box to compare and adjust one to four color components (tone, shadows, highlights, and saturation) in your photos.

Correcting and understanding color (continued)

Figure 8-5

Use the Remove Color Cast command in Standard Edit to reset and correct the color in your photos so that white, gray, and black color tones appear as expected.

Figure 8-6

A   B

C

You can change colors in an image using the Hue/Saturation command.
*A. Original **B.** Entire image changed to sepia using the Colorize option **C.** Magenta colors targeted in the Edit menu and changed using the Hue slider*

Figure 8-7

Bring out the rich vibrant colors in your photos by adjusting the hue and saturation using the Hue/Saturation command in Standard Edit.

Figure 8-8

Bring out the natural skin tones in the people in your photos, and increase the warmth of all colors in your photo by using the Adjust Color For Skin Tone command in Standard Edit. Original (top) and after adjusting for skin tone (bottom).

Retouching and transforming

Figure 10-1

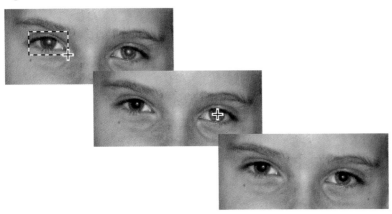

Remove red eye by using the Red Eye Removal tool and either selecting an eye (top) or clicking an eye (center).

Index

A

Adjust Hue/Saturation command 75

Adjust Skin Tone command 76

adjustment layers. *See Help*

Adobe Bridge

about 33

adjusting windows 34

Compact mode 34

displaying files and folders 35

finding files 40

keywords 38

labeling 39

main components 33

navigating files and folders 36

new windows 34

opening and closing files 33

opening files 36

organizing files 36

rating files 39

selecting files 36

viewing files and folders 35

Adobe Expert Support 1

See also Help

Adobe Help Center

about 1

adding contact information to 3

changing the view 5

displaying More Resources 3

Help topics in 3

navigating Help 3

preferences for 2

printing Help topics 5

searching Help topics 3

viewing support documents 3

Adobe Photoshop Elements

changed features 7

installing 1

new features 7

registering 1

removing 1

Adobe Premiere Elements

installing 1

registering 1

removing 1

Adobe Press 6

As Details command, Bridge 35

As Filmstrip command, Bridge 35

As Versions And Alternates command, Bridge 35

Asian type. *See Help*

auto commands 72

B

background color 97

Background layer

about 47

converting to regular layer 49

blending modes. *See Help*

bookmarks

for Help topics 5

brightness

adjusting with Levels 72

contrast and 73

Brightness/Contrast command 73

Browse command 33

Burn tool 74

C

camera raw files

about 45

fixing color 67

canceling an operation 29

canvas, resizing 79

cascade windows 28

clipboard, clearing 30

Clone Stamp tool 88

Close Window command, Bridge 34

closing

files 42

windows in Editor 28

color

about foreground and background 97

adjusting 75

adjusting for skin tone 76

adjusting saturation and hue 75

camera raw 67

changing 75

correcting 67

fixing in Quick Fix 67

fixing in Standard Edit 67, 70

color casts

adjusting with Levels 72

correcting 74

removing 75

compact mode, Bridge 34

Compact view, in Adobe Help Center 5

Compact view, of tutorials 6

completed operations alert 22

composites, Magic Extractor 60

content area, in Adobe Bridge 33

contrast, adjusting 73

Copy command, Bridge 36

copying

    areas of a photo 88

crooked images

    straightening 80

    straightening and dividing 80

Crop command 78

Crop tool 77

cropping

    Crop command 78

    Crop tool 77

Cut command, Bridge 36

D

darkening images 74

Decrease Rating command, Bridge 39

Deselect All command, Bridge 36

dialog boxes, using pop-up sliders 23

Divide Scanned Photos command 80

Dodge tool 74

double-byte type. *See Help*

downloading updates, plug-ins, and tryouts 7

downsample an image 83

Duplicate command, Bridge 36

E

Editor

    palettes 23

    printing a photo from 101

effects

    See also Help

    about 93

Eject command, Bridge 36

Elliptical Marquee tool

    options for 54

    using 54

Enhance commands 72

F

features

    changed 7

    new 7

file formats 43

files

    camera raw 45

    finding in Bridge 40

    labeling in Bridge 39

    managing in Bridge 36

    navigating in Bridge 36

    opening in Bridge 36

    rating in Bridge 39

    selecting in Bridge 36

fill layers

    converting to image layers 51

fill layers. *See Help*

Filter Gallery 94

filters

    See also Help

    about 93

    gallery 94

Find command, Bridge 40

finding files and folders, with Bridge 40

fixing

    color in Quick Fix 67

    large blemishes 88

    red eyes 87

    small blemishes with Spot Healing Brush 87

flipping a photo

    automatically 90

    manually 90

folders

    finding in Bridge 40

    navigating in Bridge 36

foreground color 97

forums 6

Free Transform 91

Full view, in Adobe Help Center 5

H

Healing Brush 88

Help system

    about 3

    navigating 3

    printing from 5

    searching 3

    updating topics 2

Help system, tutorials in 6

highlights

    adjusting with Levels 72

    adjusting with tools 74

    shadows and 73

Horizontal Type tool 99

How To palette 18

hue

    adjusting 75

    changing 75

I

image size 81

Image Size command 83

images

    opening 41

Increase Rating command, Bridge 39

installing

    instructions for 1

Inverse command 62

Invert Selection command, Bridge 36

K

keywords, applying to files in Bridge 38

L

Label commands, in Bridge 39

Lasso tool

    options for 56

    switching to Magnetic Lasso tool 57

    using 55

layer group

    about 48

    simplifying 51

layer styles

    See also Help

    about 93

layers

    about 47

    adding 49

    adding to an image 49

    converting to the Background 49

    copying 64

    deleting 51

    hiding and showing 50

    locking and unlocking 50

    renaming 51

    selecting 50

    simplifying 51

Layers palette, about 48

Levels

    about 72

lighten images 74

locked layers 50

M

Magic Extractor 60

Magic Selection Brush tool 58

Magic Wand tool

    options for 58

    using 57

Magnetic Lasso tool

    options for 57

    switching to Lasso tool 57

    using 56

magnifying

    a view 26

    and resizing 27

Marquee tool, options for 54

Match Location command 28

Match Zoom command 28

memory

    clearing from the clipboard 30

    clearing from Undo History palette 30

monitor resolution, scaling and 82

Move To Trash command, Bridge 36

Move tool

    moving selections with 64

    options for 64

    using 64

N

Navigator palette

    about 27

    zooming 26

new features 7

New Window command, Bridge 34

No Label command, Bridge 39

No Rating command, Bridge 39

O

online Help 3

online training 6

opacity. *See Help*

Open With Camera Raw command, Bridge 36

Open With command, Bridge 36

opening

    multiple windows of the same image 28

    PDF files 42

operations, undoing or redoing 30

P

painting

    about 97

    Brush tool 97

    Impressionist Brush tool 97

Palette Bin 23

palettes

    Palette Bin 23

    using in Editor 23

paragraph type 99

Paste command, Bridge 36

pasting selections 65

PDF files

    opening 42

Persistent command, Bridge 38

photos

    fitting to the screen 27

    opening multiple windows of 28

    opening one multiple times 28

reverting to previous state 30

viewing at 100% 27

Place command, Bridge 36

plug-ins

in Adobe Store 7

Polygonal Lasso tool

options for 56

using 56

pop-up palettes

about 31

working with presets 31

preferences

completed operations alert 22

file saving 45

general 27

Premiere Elements. *See* Adobe
Premiere Elements

Preset Manager

about 32

presets

about 31

in a pop-up palette 31

Preset Manager 32

print dimensions, changing 83

printer resolution 82

printing

from the Editor 101

Help topics 5

Q

Quick Fix

auto commands 72

color 67

editing photos in 67

fixing color 67

removing red eyes 87

viewing images in 25

R

rating files, in Bridge 39

Rectangular Marquee tool

options for 54

using 54

red eye

removing in Quick Fix 67

removing in Standard Edit 87

Red Eye Removal tool 87

redoing an operation 29

reducing a view 26

Refresh command, Bridge 35

registering

instructions for 1

removing

objects from a photo 87, 88

parts of a photo 77

red eye 67, 87

renaming

layers 51

resampling images 83

Reset All Tools command 22

Reset Tool command 22

resizing

automatically 27

for print 83

while zooming 27

resolution

about 81

changing 83

Reveal In Bridge command,
Bridge 36

Reveal In Explorer command,
Bridge 36

Reveal In Finder command,
Bridge 36

Revert To Saved command 30

reverting

to previous state 30

to saved version 30

rotating

by a set percentage 90

freely 90

RSS feeds 3

S

saturation

adjusting with hue 75

changing 75

saving

about 43

options 43

searching for files and folders,
Bridge 40

Select All command, Bridge 36

Select Labeled command,
Bridge 36

Select Unlabeled command,
Bridge 36

selecting

about 53

files, in Bridge 36

Magic Extractor 60

Magic Selection Brush tool 58

selection borders

moving 62

Selection Brush tool

options for 59

using 59

selection tools 53

selections

adding to 63

copying 64

deleting 62

inverting 62

moving with Move tool 64

pasting into one another 65

subtracting from 63

Send To Recycle Bin command, Bridge 36

Shadow/Highlights command 73

shadows

about 72

adjusting with tools 74

highlights and 73

shape layers

about 99

simplifying 51

shapes

See also Help

about 99

Show All Files command, Bridge 35

Show Camera Raw Files Only command, Bridge 35

Show Folders command, Bridge 35

Show Graphic Files Only command, Bridge 35

Show Hidden Files command, Bridge 35

Show Thumbnail Only command, Bridge 35

Show Vector Files Only command, Bridge 35

simplifying layers 51

skin tone, adjusting color for 76

Slideshow command, Bridge 35

software

downloads 7

registering 1

updating 2

Sort command, Bridge 35

Spot Healing Brush 87

Standard Edit

auto commands 72

fixing color 67, 70

viewing images 25

workflow 70

stars, rating files with in Bridge 39

straightening images

and separating 80

single images 80

Styles And Effects palette, using 93

superimposing, using the Magic Extractor 60

support documents, in Adobe Help Center 2

support options 6

See also Help

system requirements

about 1

T

technical support

See also Help

Adobe Expert Support 1

complimentary and paid 6

on Adobe.com 6

text. *See* type

tile windows 28

tonal range, adjusting 72

toolbox

about 20

selecting a tool 20

tools

See also individual tool names

options 22

preferences 20

training resources 6

transforming

layers 91

photos 91

selections 91

tryouts 7

tutorials 9

type

See also Help

entering 99

tools 99

type layers

creating 99

simplifying 51

U

undo 29

Undo History palette

clearing memory 30

deleting states 30

using 29

Unfiltered menu, Bridge 35

updates 7

updating

software and Help topics 2

user forums 6

V

vector graphics

creating shapes 99

Vertical Type tool 99

viewing

fit to the screen 27

multiple windows 28

multiple windows of the same image 28

navigating in window 27

photos at 100% 27

photos in Quick Fix 25

photos in Standard Edit 25

print size 82

tiled windows 28

views

in Adobe Help Center 5

W

Welcome Screen 15

windows

closing 28

magnifying 27

opening multiple of same
image 28

resizing 27

tile 28

workspace

about 20

Welcome Screen 15

Z

zooming

and resizing 27

in Editor 26